Pearls
Scriptural Truths
Revealed

SANDRA S. WILLIAMS

ISBN:0615444113
ISBN-13: 9780615444116

PRAYER OF EMPOWERMENT

Father God, I pray abundant blessings over the life of your people. Lord I ask that you will strengthen us to walk worthy of the vocation that you've called us to. Empower us to walk in the anointing and authority that you've placed in our lives. Lead and guide us into all truth. Let every word spoken from our lips bring you glory. Remove every hindrance, obstacle, snare, and trap that the enemy tries to put in our way, and if you don't remove it, God I pray that you will give us the ability to conquer it. For you said in your word...we are more than conquerors. We are overcomers. We have the victory already.

I pray that you will give us the insight and revelation knowledge needed to advance the kingdom and to empower others to walk upright before you. I pray that you will give us a mind to want to live a holy and set apart life...a life of holiness....A life dedicated and completely committed to you. I pray that you will continue to build us up and give us spiritual maturity, insight and depth. I pray that as we grow that you will raise us up to declare your great works to this lost nation.

Lord increase in us as we decrease. Dismiss, delete and deny anything that is not like you from our lives. Let us remain sober, vigilant and watchful. Let us guard our hearts and minds so that no evil will overtake us. Lord thank you for your divine protection. Thank you for instilling in us the value of prayer and daily supplication of your word. Lord as we learn more about you we ask that you will bless us to utilize what we've learned to advance your kingdom and empower the next generation. Lord we worship you on today. We magnify and glorify your holy name. We lift you up and exalt you Lord God. For you are all powerful. You are a mighty God. You are the Prince of Peace. You are the King of Kings. You make a way when we can't see the way. You conquered death, raised the dead, you heal the sick, open blinded eyes, and you're a strong deliverer. You're a mighty fortress. You're a present help in the time of trouble. You're everything God and we stand before you humble...giving you all praise...all glory....we reverence you God. We adore you. We love you. You are our Savior and we are forever grateful for all that you've done; for all that you're going to do; and yet Lord we praise you if you don't do anything else for us...because we know you're able. God you are great and greatly to be praised. Cleanse our lips, our hearts, and our minds. Cleanse us God and make us ready. Prepare us God for your use, for your glory, for your purpose. We yield our lives to you God...completely. Thank you for your sacrifice that afforded us the opportunity to live abundantly. Amen

CONTENTS

Acknowledgements   I

Pearls of Hope & Encouragement   1

Pearls of Wisdom & Guidance   50

Pearls of Enlightenment   68

Pearls of Warning   86

Pearls of Exposure & Illumination   124

Pearls of Patience & Endurance   159

****Scriptures derived from the KJV unless otherwise noted****

Sandra S. Williams

ACKNOWLEDGMENTS

I first and foremost would like to acknowledge my Lord and Savior Jesus Christ for imparting the wisdom, revelation and knowledge to create this project. I would like to thank my husband Mr. Markus Williams for always pushing me and motivating me to not give up on writing this book. I also would like to acknowledge my Mother Ms. Bessie Williams for raising me to be a "Woman of God". Lastly but certainly not least, I would like to thank my children for always holding me up in prayer and for always believing in me.

ACKNOWLEDGMENTS

PEARLS OF HOPE & ENCOURAGMENT

"COME HOME"

(Return To Your First Love)

Scriptural Emphasis:

"That is why the LORD says, 'Turn to me now, while there is time. Give me your hearts. Come with fasting, weeping, and mourning. Don't tear your clothing in your grief, but tear your hearts instead.' Return to the LORD your God, for he is merciful and compassionate, slow to get angry and filled with unfailing love." Joel 2:12-13

Are you tired of running aimlessly thru life looking for the next popular fad to attach yourself to? Are you tired of succumbing to the things of this world? Are you tired of where you are; what you're doing; and how you're living? I have the ultimate answer for you today. Return home! God has need of you.

True repentance is what God is calling for. The word repent means (according to Webster) to turn from sin and dedicate oneself to the amendment of one's life; to feel regret or contrition; to change one's mind; to feel sorrowful.

My sacrifice [the sacrifice acceptable] to God is a broken spirit; a broken and a contrite heart [broken down with sorrow for sin and humbly and thoroughly penitent], such, O God, You will not despise. (Psalms 51:17 Amplified)

True repentance is not merely about your outward appearance but more importantly repentance is about your heart; for the outward appearance of a man or woman are most times deceiving but God examines and judges the heart. The scripture above states that the acceptable sacrifice to God is a broken (burst or torn) spirit: a broke and contrite heart...a heart that has sorrowfully collapsed and has now become humble through repentance. This sacrifice God will not despise but honor.

Repentance is not just an outward change. Joel commanded and instructed Israel to fast, weep and mourn (outward actions) but repentance took place in the turning, rending and returning. Anyone can change their clothes and appear to be holy but what matters to God is that your heart is completely turned to Him.

If my people, who are called by My name, shall humble themselves, pray,(seek, crave, and require of necessity) My face and turn from their wicked ways, then will I hear from heaven, forgive their sin, and heal their land. (2 Chronicles 7:14 Amp)

Looking closely at this scripture; It does not say if my people who are called by My name would change their clothes and put on a mask to appear sorrowful and grieved over the sins they've committed....but it says that one should turn...reverse your course and direction from your wicked ways. Repentance means you've committed to changing your position. It means you've defected from the side you once were committed to; but now you've repositioned yourself to the winning side...God's side.

True repentance will revoke the sentence God has place on the life of a sinner. Let's take a look and see what takes place when true repentance occurs.

[5]So the people of Nineveh believed in God and proclaimed a fast and put on sackcloth [in penitent mourning], from the greatest of them even to the least of them.

[6]For word came to the king of Nineveh [of all that had happened to Jonah, and his terrifying message from God], and he arose from his throne and he laid his robe aside, covered himself with sackcloth, and sat in ashes.

[7]And he made proclamation and published through Nineveh, By the decree of the king and his nobles: Let neither man nor beast, herd nor flock, taste anything; let them not feed nor drink water.

[8]But let man and beast be covered with sackcloth and let them cry mightily to God. Yes, let everyone turn from his evil way and from the violence that is in his hands.

[9]Who can tell, God may turn and revoke His sentence against us [when we have met His terms], and turn away from His fierce anger so that we perish not.

[10]And God saw their works, that they turned from their evil way; and God revoked His [sentence of] evil that He had said that He would do to them and He did not do it [for He was comforted and eased concerning them]. (Jonah 3:5-10 KJV)

God is calling for true repentance. You may have strayed away from God, but God is calling you; beckoning for you to return to Him. He's patiently waiting on you to choose life by accepting Him as your Lord and Savior. As the prodigal son returned home to his father; sorrowful and with deep regret, so must we return to God rending our hearts, repentant and ashamed; then and only then can we rest in the loving arms of Jesus and stand before Him forgiven.

But if we walk in the light, as he is in the light, we have fellowship one with another, and the blood of Jesus Christ his Son cleanseth us from all sin. (1 John 1:7KJV)

PRAYER OF EMPOWERMENT:

Father, I stand broken in spirit, sorrowful and with sincere regret asking you to pardon my sins. Father I ask that you will cleanse me from the inside out and make me to stand in right fellowship with you. Forgive me for living contrary to your word. Strengthen me to walk upright before you and to live a life of humility. Father, I thank you for allowing me to return home; to you my first love.

Amen

PAUSE, REWIND, FAST FORWARD, & LIVE!

SCRIPTURAL EMPHASIS:

[9] We can make our plans, but the LORD determines our steps. (Psalms 16:9)

Sometimes the answer to your prayer is simply on pause…God has merely pressed pause to give you the opportunity to press rewind and repent…so He can then press fast forward and give you your reward. What are you doing while God has you on "pause?" Your response to "pause" will dictate when you'll be advanced to the next level. In the pause season you must persistently pursue God with prayer, worship and praise. God puts you on "pause" because He's trying to get you to see something important. There's something in the "pause" moment being unveiled that you cannot afford to miss.

It's just like watching a good suspense movie that in order for you to figure out everything that's going on, you have to be attentive to every detail; and in that moment when critical information is about to be unveiled you have to go to the bathroom or the phone rings. You hit pause because you don't want to miss key information. Pause allows you the opportunity to meditate and reflect. If we take a look in Psalms we see many scriptures that at the end of the verse there was an opportunity to pause and reflect. The terminology used in the scriptures that define pause is Selah. Whenever you see the word Selah; it is saying now meditate and absorb what you've just read. Let it marinate and sink in.

At times you will have to hit "rewind" to go back and take a closer look. It's what I call a "hold up" moment. You know when you're watching something and it goes by so fast that you say…wait a minute…hold up…rewind that….it's a moment of clarification. So in life God may hit the "rewind" button to clarify a few things…to also give you an opportunity to repent of anything that will stand in your way of obtaining the promise; to show you the error of your way; to correct you so you can continue moving forward. It's when you're in the rewind mode that you feel you'll never get to where God wants you to be…it's in the rewind season that you feel insignificant, unqualified, incompetent and inept. But it's actually in this season that God is repairing, rebuilding, reviving, and restoring you to your rightful place in Him. It's in the rewind stage that you're being made over again.

The prefix "re" means to do again; to make anew. The word "rewind" according to Webster's definition means to reverse the winding. "Wind" means to turn the course of; to lead to a desired destination or end result. Delving into the word rewind…it simply means to turn the course of which will lead to a desired place or end result; to make new; to do again. The word of God even tells us that when we veer off the desired course that God has provided that we are to return and do our first works again.

Revelation 2:5 (Amplified Bible) *⁵Remember then from what heights you have fallen. Repent (change the inner man to meet God's will) and do the works you did previously [when first you knew the Lord], or else I will visit you and remove your lamp stand from its place, unless you change your mind and repent.*

You must re-examine and re-visit the place where you were when you were truly sold out and on fire for the Lord. You must re-do the very things that it took to gain a close and more intimate relationship with Christ all over again.

Once you've paused (meditated and absorbed), re-winded (repented, made anew, reversed the order) you can then expect

9

God to hit "fast forward". This phase allows you to skip over and bypass what would have once caught you off guard and caused you to falter. It will catapult you from the end of the line to the forefront. The word "forward" as defined by Webster states: situated in advance; notably advanced or developed; moving, tending, or leading toward a position in the front. When we follow the course that God has designated for our lives we will ultimately move from the back to the front. The word of God puts it like this….Deuteronomy28:13 (KJV) *¹³And the LORD shall make thee the head, and not the tail; and thou shalt be above only, and thou shalt not be beneath; if that thou hearken unto the commandments of the LORD thy God, which I command thee this day, to observe and to do them:*

So don't be dismayed or fret when you find yourself on pause or rewind; because if you obey the word of the Lord and allow God to lead you and guide thru this journey…your end resolve will catapult you into your promised destiny.

PRAYER OF EMPOWERMENT:

Father, thank you for pressing "pause" in my life; for showing me that in the "pause" season I must reflect, meditate on the things that will advance me to the next level. Lord, thank you for pressing "rewind" in my life; giving me the opportunity to repent and re-do my first works over; to gain a closer relationship with you. Finally Lord, thank you for pressing "fast forward" in my life; catapulting me to the next level in you; allowing me to bypass the pitfalls that the devil has setup. Thank you God for showing me that in order for me to be above and not beneath; the head and not the tail; the lender and not the borrower that I must endure the "pause" and "rewind" seasons; for it is in these seasons that my relationship with you is repaired, restored and revived. Amen

"IT WON'T PROSPER"

SCRIPTURAL EMPHASIS:

No weapon that is formed against thee shall prosper; and every tongue that shall rise against thee in judgment thou shalt condemn. This is the heritage of the servants of the LORD, and their righteousness is of me, saith the LORD. Isaiah 54:17

The main agenda of the enemy is to steal, kill, and destroy. (John 10:10) He wants to rob you of your time, energy, gifts, callings and talents. So to do this he must devise a plan to take you out. Make no mistake about it, the enemy can't stand you. He despises you and your determination to live for Christ. He refuses to allow anything to exalt itself above him. He plots and schemes on those who he feel can damage his kingdom. His job is to stop your confession of Jesus Christ.

The enemy is certainly on his job so we too must be on ours. He will use anything to knock you off course and alter your destiny. We must cognizant of his plots and schemes. We must readily recognize when things seem to be out of sync that it's the plot of the enemy. The enemy is on the prowl seeking those he can devour. We must always maintain an increased level of alertness so we can foil the plot of the enemy.

When God has you on assignment, it is the enemy's job to hinder and or cancel that assignment. One of his focal points is to attack your mind. He will begin to plant seeds of doubt and insecurity. He'll tell you that you're not qualified or equipped to carry out the assignment, but we must dismiss these implanted thoughts that the enemy will bring or we will abort the mission that God has authorized and ordained.

Nehemiah chapter four tells a story of how the enemy was on assignment to stop the wall that was being built which in return would stop him. When word got out that this wall was being erected the enemy became infuriated to the point that he launched a plot to halt it. But the part of this story I love is when the enemy found out the people were fully aware of the plot against them. The NIV version of Nehemiah 4:15-16 tells us that God frustrated the enemy's plot which put the builders on alert…some built while others were on security detail.

Although God spoiled the plot of the enemy the people still had to have an increased level of attentiveness, diligence, and readiness to ensure the assignment was completed.

We must apply this to our lives even more so every single day, because we do not fight a physical enemy. The bible tells us in 2 Corinthians 10 verse 4 that the weapons of our warfare are not carnal, but mighty through God to the pulling down of strong holds. Ephesians 6:12 further states, we are not wrestling with flesh and blood [contending only with physical opponents], but against the despotisms, against the powers, against [the master spirits who are] the world rulers of this present darkness, against the spirit forces of wickedness in the heavenly (supernatural) sphere. (Amplified)

So we must remain alert while continuing to build the Kingdom of God….not just relying on our physical strength, but more importantly the Word of God. We must be aware yet fully confident that the weapons will form, but they will not prosper.

Prayer of Empowerment:

Lord, as we continue on the assignments you've placed us on, let us keep our eyes focused on you. Help us to maintain a high level of alertness and awareness of the enemy's plot to abort our divine assignments. Strengthen us with the fortitude to stand and continue to build your kingdom. Guard our hearts and minds against the seeds of doubt & insecurity that the enemy will try to plant. Help us to stand on your word that although the weapon is formed…it won't prosper.

Amen

PROMISES

SCRIPTURAL EMPHASIS:

For all the promises of God in him are yea, and in him Amen, unto the glory of God by us. 1 Corinthians 1:20

God is a faithful, just and true God. Everything God says is guaranteed and sealed in the blood. We never have to worry about the validity of God's promises. If He said it, it will come to pass. If He makes a promise to you, He will make good on His promises. God cannot and will not break His word. Man will make promises, but will very seldom follow through with them. The reliability of man is unstable, but the reliability of God is solid and sound. God has consistently kept His promises. Man has the capability to fail; but in God there is no failure.

And, behold, this day I am going the way of all the earth: and ye know in all your hearts and in all your souls, that not one thing hath failed of all the good things which the LORD your God spake concerning you; all are come to pass unto you, and not one thing hath failed thereof. (Joshua 23:14 KJV)

God is the only one you can put your trust in totally because God cannot fail. God will not promise you something and then decide to renege on that promise. God does not change His mind. He doesn't have amnesia or short term memory. The faithfulness of God cannot be challenged or questioned. God is faithful. He will

make good on His promises. All we must do is believe what He says.

God is not a man, that he should lie; neither the son of man, that he should repent: hath he said, and shall he not do it? Or hath he spoken, and shall he not make it good? (Numbers 23:19 KJV)

If God said it, it's a done deal. The matter is settled. God is incapable of lying. It's not in His nature. He's a God of truth. You can count on God's promises.

There are many examples of the promises of God in the Bible, but I want to take a look at seven promises that God has made to man.

#1 God promised to meet our needs. God is our provision. God is who provides our every need.

But my God shall supply all your need according to his riches in glory by Christ Jesus. (Philippians 4:19 KJV)

The scripture doesn't state that God will supply our wants, but more importantly He will supply are needs. But the awesome thing about God is that every now and then he sprinkles some of our wants in with our needs. Who wouldn't serve a God like this?

#2 God promised us sufficient grace.

And he said unto me, My grace is sufficient for thee: for my strength is made perfect in weakness. (2 Corinthians 12:9a KJV)

Grace has been described and defined as God's unmerited favor. It has also been broken down acronymically as God's Riches at Christ Expense. Simply put, grace is getting what we don't deserve. We aren't worthy of the grace of God but God gives it to us anyway.

#3 God promised that temptation will not overtake us.

There hath no temptation taken you but such as is common to man: but God is faithful, who will not suffer you to be tempted above that ye are able; but will with the temptation also make a way to escape, that ye may be able to bear it. (1 Corinthians 10:13)

For in that He Himself has suffered, being tempted, He is able to aid those who are tempted.(Hebrews 2:18 NKJV)

It's reassuring to know that when we are tempted that God has provided a way of escape for us. Temptation will come, but we do not have to succumb to it. We are not exempt from being tempted. Just as Christ was tempted; we too will face temptation, but God promised us that when we are tempted He will provide a way out.

#4 God promised us victory over sin and death.

But thank God! He gives us victory over sin and death through our Lord Jesus Christ. (1 Corinthians 15:57 NLT)

We all know that sin leads to destruction and death. But God has promised us victory over sin and death. If we walk according to the word of God and live a lifestyle of holiness we have victory over death. As long as we walk after the spirit and deny our flesh the pleasures of sin, we have the victory. Christ died on the cross for our sins, but he rose with all power in His hands and victory over death. Death could not hold Him. The grave could not retain or detain Him. He got up so we can get up.

#5 God promised us that all things will work together.

And we know that all things work together for good to them that love God, to them who are the called according to his purpose. (Romans 8:28 KJV)

God will cause all things to work on our behalf for our good through our love for Him. He has called us according to His divine purpose and plan for His glory. The enemy wants to do us harm, destroy us and ultimately kill us, but God wants to protect us and preserve us for His use. God is always in control therefore we have nothing to fear.

Joseph replied, "Don't be afraid. Do I act for God? Don't you see, you planned evil against me but God used those same plans for my good, as you see all around you right now—life for many people. Easy now, you have nothing to fear; I'll take care of you and your children." He reassured them, speaking with them heart-to-heart. (Genesis 50:20 Message)

#6 God promises salvation.

He that believeth and is baptized shall be saved; but he that believeth not shall be damned. (Mark 16:16 KJV)

That if thou shalt confess with thy mouth the Lord Jesus, and shalt believe in thine heart that God hath raised him from the dead, thou shalt be saved. [10]For with the heart man believeth unto righteousness; and with the mouth confession is made unto salvation. (Romans 10:9-10 KJV)

Our confession is the first step to salvation. Confess it; believe it; receive it. Sin separated us from God. God loved us so much that He gave His only son to die on the cross for our sins. He suffered so we wouldn't have to suffer. He died to give us life and not just life but abundant life. He got up to show us that you can overcome anything; nothing can hold you back. We must dedicate our life to holiness. We must walk according to the spirit of God. We must yield ourselves completely to God. Confession is only part of salvation, but once we receive Christ we must work out our salvation. It's a daily walk of faith.

#7 God promises us eternal life.

My sheep hear my voice, and I know them, and they follow me:
[28]And I give unto them eternal life; and they shall never perish,
neither shall any man pluck them out of my hand. (John 10:27-28)

Life on earth is temporary. Time does not stand still. Years no longer feel like years but more like months. Months seem like days, and days seem like mere hours. Each year goes by quicker than the previous year. Our time on earth is limited, but if belong to Christ we are guaranteed eternal life with Him. If we remain obedient to God; we will gain eternal life.

He that believeth on the Son hath everlasting life: and he that believeth not the Son shall not see life; but the wrath of God abideth on him. (John 3:36 KJV)

There are a vast amount of God's promises in the word of God. All we have to do is be obedient and faithful to Him and He will be faithful to us. We are to live a yielded and surrendered life to God, and He promised that no good thing would He withhold from us as long as we walk upright before Him.

For the LORD God is a sun and shield: the LORD will give grace and glory: no good thing will he withhold from them that walk uprightly. (Psalms 84:11 KJV)

PRAYER OF EMPOWERMENT:

Father, thank you for being a faithful and just God. Thank you for every promise you've made to us, for we know that they are yes and amen in you. Lord, thank you for your grace, provision, love, and mercy. Thank you for showing us your agape love by giving your only begotten son as the sacrificial lamb; the one who died on the cross for our sins; the one who has afforded us the right to eternal life. Empower us to walk in obedience daily so that we will not forfeit our position in the Kingdom. Empower us to walk upright before you and to be found pleasing in your sight. Thank you for your sacrifice; for covering us under the blood; for redeeming us from the curse of the law. Thank you for being merciful toward us. We don't take your sacrifice for granted but we praise you and glorify you for all that you've done for us. Amen

"REMNANTS"

SCRIPTURAL EMPHASIS:

A remnant will return; yes, the remnant of Jacob will return to the Mighty God. Isaiah 10:21

As this topic dropped in my spirit I immediately related the word remnant with leftovers. I have fond memories of observing my mother prepare dinner for four as if she was about to feed an entire army. When asked if we were having guest over for dinner the answer was no, "I'm making enough to have leftovers." As I was reminiscing about my childhood and the many times we had leftovers it led me to discover its value. It's funny because although the initial meal was freshly prepared and delicious, it was even better the next day. The seasoning had time to marinate which offered a boost of flavor that wasn't necessarily initially present. So let's apply this to the Word of God....

Week after week we sit in our Sunday morning worship services and weeknight bible studies looking to receive a word from God. Each week the Praise Team emerges to set an atmosphere where the word can come forth. We sit as if we're at our dinner tables....bibles spread open, writing utensil in hand, hearts, minds and ears open to receive a much needed word. The man or woman of God has spent countless hours in prayer and consecration to deliver the word that God has spoken to him or her. We sit attentively listening to what thus says the Lord through the vessel He's chosen for that appointed time. The word goes forth and throughout the course of the message you may hear an Amen, or go ahead and preach. Sometimes you may even hear…"now that's good" or "say that again". You know kind of how when the natural meal is getting good to us we say things like, "this is delicious, this food will make you slap somebody or sometimes it's complete silence that takes over because the food is just too good to say anything. You just want to enjoy it until the last bite is devoured so you can sit back rubbing your stomach letting what you've just consumed digest. The next day you go rummaging through the refrigerator looking for what you consumed the day before because you've been thinking about it non-stop. There may be only a few bites left but you must have more…you've been craving it all day.

I can imagine hearing you say, "I can't wait to get home because the meal I had on yesterday is waiting for me today."

That's the way the Word of God is. When God imparts a Word into your life you want to feast on that Word not just the day it's imparted but you want the remnant of that Word to spill over day after day. When you're going thru a midnight experience you want to be able to go and pull some joy from the Word you received. When you can't seem to find your way, you can pull out, "he leads me in the paths of righteousness". When the enemy is hot on your tracks you can pull out, "No weapon formed against me shall prosper". (Isaiah 54:17a) You may not be able to remember every word that was spoken but there's a remnant that was left in the recesses of your mind that no matter what you face that word will manifest itself and speak life to your situation. When you've cried and cried because nothing seems to be going your way, you can pull from the remnant, "Weeping may endure for a night, but joy cometh in the morning." (Psalms 30:5) You may never be a Bible scholar or a Theologian. You may never read the Bible from cover to cover or memorize every scripture, but there will always be a "remnant" word that's marinating in your heart and mind, waiting to be recalled at the right time for the right situation. Don't throw away the leftovers. They are just as useful if not more useful than the complete meal. I remember when my Mother would cook a ham and after we've devoured it….and we think it's of no more value and will need to be discarded of…my Mother would say…"don't throw that bone away" I'm going to use that to season my greens. It's amazing to me that the things we think are of no use or are insignificant can be used to season and bring a desired taste to a bland situation.

Sometimes we go to church and we don't feel like praising God. We've been through hell all week long…and we feel we don't have a praise to offer. But I beg to differ…deep in the recesses of your heart there's a remnant praise left over. All you have to do is think back…Ah…Just thinking on the goodness of Jesus and the awesome things he's done for you, resurrects a thunderous praise that was sitting in storage left over from when you came out of the fire two weeks ago. That thing that was meant to destroy you and take your life couldn't because that remnant word you stored away stepped in and said "I shall not die, but live, and declare the works of the LORD. (Psalms 118:7)

Just as the body needs nourishment; we must also feed our spirit man. We should ensure that we build up our spiritual man by nourishing it daily with the Word of God; realizing we may not memorize it word for word but that there will be a remnant left over that will build our faith and strengthen us during our times of adversity.

PRAYER OF EMPOWERMENT:

Father, I thank you for the remnants. I thank you for the things others think are of no use and insignificant, but are actually instrumental in my healing, deliverance and restoration. I pray for your guidance and wisdom for every aspect of my life. Empower me to utilize the remnants to overcome every obstacle. I realize what I digest today will be instrumental in my survival tomorrow. Amen

"THE MANTLE"

(The Blessing of a Double Portion)

Scriptural Emphasis:

2 Kings 2:8-14

Key Verses: 2 Kings 2:14-15

And he took the mantle of Elijah that fell from him, and smote the waters, and said, Where is the LORD God of Elijah? And when he also had smitten the waters, they parted hither and thither: and Elisha went over.

And when the sons of the prophets which were to view at Jericho saw him, they said, the spirit of Elijah doth rest on Elisha. And they came to meet him, and bowed themselves to the ground before him.

Before we can delve into the end result of Elisha receiving the mantle that was on Elijah, we must first understand that it wasn't just handed to him...he earned it. Some tend to think that blessings should be handed to them on a silver platter. They think it's a given that they should have only the best. In the natural sense some tend to believe they are automatically deserving of whatever they desire and all they need do is ask for it. But they fail to realize that in order to receive one must first give. The principle of giving to receive is presented all throughout the Bible. The Bible even goes far enough to tell us that faith without works is dead. What does this mean? It means your faith cannot be activated without some action on your part.

God chose Elisha to follow Elijah. During their journey Elisha served and worked closely with Elijah. This is what I believe to be a divine appointment for Elisha. It's safe to say that Elisha was in training. During their journey together several miracles were wrought. Elisha wasn't just a side-kick. On the contrary, Elisha was on a divine assignment which would result in him being in position for the transference of the great power and anointing Elijah possessed to one day rest on him. It wasn't just handed to him...he followed Elijah as a servant. He was faithful to Elijah. Where Elijah went...Elisha went. He didn't leave him when trouble broke out. He didn't quit when things became too complex. He refused to leave his side.

When it was time for Elijah to leave, he asked of Elisha what he could do for him, and Elisha stated, I desire to have a double portion of your spirit. Elijah told Elisha that he had asked a hard thing of him. Which says to me, you're asking for something that has some prerequisites? This won't be an easy thing to do, but Elijah gave Elisha clear instruction for Elisha to keep his eyes on him when the time came that he was taken up so his desire would come to pass. This also lets me know, you can't be off doing your own thing...you must be with me to receive what I have. Don't ask for something you're not willing to commit to getting. If the blessing is with me...then you must be with me to get it.

(2 Kings 2:10 - And he said, Thou hast asked a hard thing: nevertheless, if thou see me when I am taken from thee, it shall be so unto thee; but if not, it shall not be so.)

God is telling us the same thing....if we can keep our eyes focused on HIM, we can have the desires of our hearts. We can't expect to receive more anointing by sitting on our seats of do nothing. There's work involved in receiving the blessings of God. We must be faithful in the work of the Lord. We must commit ourselves to this walk whole-heartedly. We must endure a few things in order to receive a double portion. We must be able to withstand tests and trials, and endure hardship as a good soldier. We cannot bail out when things get hard. We can't give up when things don't go our way. We must follow Christ closely and garner a closer relationship with Him. We won't receive any fruit if we haven't labored. The wind may blow, the waters may become turbulent, the fire may get hotter but we must remain steadfast and unmovable.

Let me stress, that Elisha didn't ask for a double portion of Elijah's spirit for his own personal reasons and gain. He didn't ask for a double portion just so he could flaunt it in someone's face. He didn't ask for a double portion just so he could stick out his chest. He however wanted to continue the work of Elijah. He wanted to continue the work of the Lord. He wanted to do great exploits for God. It was never about him, but it was always about God. So God granted Elisha's request and Elisha went on to perform far more miracles than that of Elijah, because it wasn't about his agenda, but it was always about God's agenda.

When we ask God for more power, more anointing, success and wealth, we should look closely at our motives. When our motive is pure and our desire will glorify God and not self; He will often answer in ways our imaginations cannot contain. When you ask God for more he requires more from you.

PRAYER OF EMPOWERMENT:

Father as we seek more of you, strengthen us to endure hardness. Strengthen us to follow after you with complete commitment. Father we ask that you will lead us and guide our every step. When we are faced with difficulty, we ask that you will give us the fortitude to forge ahead. Lord, protect us along the way; equipping us with everything we need to succeed in life. Make us ready to receive more of your power and anointing. Lord for we simply desire more of you.

Amen

S-T-R-E-T-C-H OUT

SCRIPTURAL EMPHASIS: Mark 3:1-5 NIV

Another time he went into the synagogue, and a man with a shriveled hand was there. [2]Some of them were looking for a reason to accuse Jesus, so they watched him closely to see if he would heal him on the Sabbath. [3]Jesus said to the man with the shriveled hand, "Stand up in front of everyone." [4]Then Jesus asked them, "Which is lawful on the Sabbath: to do good or to do evil, to save life or to kill?" But they remained silent. [5]He looked around at them in anger and, deeply distressed at their stubborn hearts, said to the man, "Stretch out your hand." He stretched it out, and his hand was completely restored.

This particular story is very encouraging to me. As we delve into this deeper my hope is that you will activate your faith and trust God for complete healing and deliverance. As I was being reared up in the church I always heard the church defined as many things, one of which was a hospital. I was taught that if you had an illness, physical or emotional the church was the place to be. James 5:14 says, Is any sick among you? Let him call for the elders of the church; and let them pray over him, anointing him with oil in the name of the Lord.

The church has long been a place of healing, deliverance and restoration. Here we see a man enter the church with a disability. He wasn't physically whole, but he was in the right place at the right time. Now before the man could receive what he came for he was met with resistance. You must know when God is about to bless you; resistance will meet you, and obstacles

28

will form. But in order to receive the blessings of God you must overcome every obstacle. You must be persistent and tenacious to obtain the blessings of God. Don't allow the distractions of people deter you from stretching out and receiving your healing.

But what I love about this story is that in spite of those that were standing waiting to see if Jesus would break the law and heal on the Sabbath Jesus yet performed a miracle on his behalf. That actually speaks volumes. It tells me that no matter what day of the week it is, no matter the obstacle, no matter the people who place opposition in your way, Jesus is always attainable. You can reach out to Christ and He will reach out to you. In spite of all of the distractions, Jesus called this man forth and told him to stand up in front of everyone. Most of us would have been fearful. We would have possibly acted as if we were okay and that we had it all together. It took an activation of faith on his part to do as Jesus commanded him to do.

Then to add more anxiety for this man, Jesus turned and asked those who were there to distract and judge, was it better to do good or evil on the Sabbath; to kill or save a life? He in fact if I may was putting them on blast, but they uttered not a word. I mean really what's more important here? Jesus simply told the man to stretch out his hand and as soon as he stretched it out he was healed.

It would have been easy for this man to run out when he was faced with opposition. But when you need something from God; when you're tired of being spiritually and physically handicapped and disabled; tired of dealing with your affliction; you have to go after what you need no matter what. When you're ready to be whole, you must activate your faith and stretch out to God and allow Him to heal you. Don't let discouragement and doubt set in. You must always remember that there is nothing too hard for God. If God said it, He will do it. If He can turn water into wine, raise the dead, cast out demonic spirits, open the blinded eye, He also can and will heal you.

Activate your faith and stretch out...God is waiting to deliver, restore and heal you. No matter what your disability, issue, weakness or circumstance is...Stretch it out...let God heal it today!

PRAYER OF EMPOWERMENT:

Father God as I activate my faith and stretch out my hand to you, I believe that you will take my hand and make me whole. Strengthen me to overcome every obstacle and distraction that comes to stand between me and my healing. Let me not be fearful to cry out to you and ask you to heal, deliver and restore. Lord, my faith is activated and I stretch out to you God...take my hand and make me whole.

Amen

ALLOS PARAKLETOS

"The Ever Abiding Spirit Within You"

SCRIPTURAL EMPHASIS:

[16]And I will ask the Father and He will give you another Comforter (Counselor, Helper, Intercessor, Advocate, Strengthener, and Standby), that He may remain with you forever-- [17]The Spirit of Truth, Whom the world cannot receive (welcome, take to its heart), because it does not see Him or know and recognize Him. But you know and recognize Him, for He lives with you [constantly] and will be in you. (John 14:16-17 Amplified)

Have you ever been so low that you couldn't even pray to God? Have you ever been in a near death situation where you couldn't find the strength to call out to God for help? Well, I have! There have been times when I couldn't pray. Not because I didn't want to, but because my situation had literally choked the words from my mouth. It's then that I had to rely on the Allos Parakletos (The Holy Spirit).

There have been times where I literally wanted to take my life. I had gone through enough. I was overwhelmed by the cares of life and it seemed as though when one thing went wrong ten more bad things followed. I told myself I was done. I couldn't take it anymore. I wanted out. I reasoned with myself that if I was dead and gone my pain would cease...and my struggle would be over. I felt abandoned and forsaken. No one understood my plight or my pain. I felt no one even cared. I just wanted to make what I was going through stop. But that wasn't the plan God had in store for my life. When I was at the end of the rope...barely

31

hanging on by the tips of my fingernails....The Allos Parakletos showed up and interceded on my behalf.

The word Parakletos means, Holy Spirit, Comforter, Advocate, Counselor, Helper, Strengthener, Intercessor, & one who pleads another's call. Allos simply means another. The word of God tells us in John 14 that we wouldn't be left here alone, but that we would be sent "another" comforter that would abide with us forever. How comforting is this to know that Jesus didn't leave us here to fend for ourselves but He sent one that would dwell on the inside of us forever.

As we look at the definition of Parakletos, it's encouraging to know that we have an Advocate with the Father; one who will intercede on our behalf; one who will be our helper and our strength in the time of trouble. When all hell is breaking loose in our lives, The Allos Parakletos is there pleading our cause. When we can't pray for ourselves, the Allos Parakletos steps in and intercedes for us. When we've exhausted every effort and can't seem to take another step, the Allos Parakletos will be strength for us. We're not alone. We have an advocate that is working on our behalf. When you feel like life has hit you in the gut one too many times and you're ready to give up, that's when the Allos Parakletos steps in and gives you the strength to keep moving forward.

No matter what you're going through; No matter how hard things may get; No matter how bleak the situation may appear; The Allos Parakletos is with us, pleading our cause, strengthening us to endure, interceding for us, providing the help we urgently need. Whatever you need...The Allos Parakletos is. He abides within you. There's nothing the Holy Spirit can't handle. He's a very present help in the time of trouble. It doesn't matter what it is...He's present in your situation. Go ahead! Rejoice in knowing that you are not alone. The Allos Parakletos is with you and abides in you.

PRAYER OF EMPOWERMENT:

Father, I thank you for sending the "Allos" (another) "Parakletos" our (Comforter, Advocate, Helper, Strengthener, and Intercessor). Help me to rely completely on the Holy Spirit to lead and guide me. I rejoice in knowing that I am not alone; for your spirit abides within me.

Amen

BAAL-PERAZIM

(The Lord Who Breaks Out)

SCRIPTURAL EMPHASIS:

1 Chronicles 14:11 (New International Version)

[11] So David and his men went up to Baal Perazim, and there he defeated them. He said, "As waters break out, God has broken out against my enemies by my hand." So that place was called Baal Perazim.

I've recently began an in-depth study on the life of David. In my studies I ran across a passage of scripture that told the story of David's defeat of the Philistines. What's key to note about this event is that David was sought out by his enemies. They in today's terms had placed an A.P.B (All Points Bulletin) out to find out where David was. When David found out that there was an inquiry regarding his whereabouts, David didn't wait on them to find him, but he in turn went out to find them. However, before he went out to find them, David asked God if He was going to hand his enemies over to him, and God spoke to David and said He would indeed. So David went up to Baal-Perazim and there he defeated the enemy. David then said, "As waters break out, God has broken out against my enemies by my hand. Oh what a mighty God we serve!

34

Let me encourage you that no matter what you're going through, God is the God of the breakout. When your enemies seek you out to destroy you, you can call on the God of the breakout. When you're inundated with tests and trials, you can depend on the God of the breakout to break you out of that situation. Just as Paul and Silas were thrown in jail; they did not allow that situation to control them. No instead they took control of the situation. They didn't lie down and die. They didn't surrender to the enemy. No! Instead they had a praise party; they prayed and sang praises to the God of the breakout. Their praise and prayers were so thunderous that it invoked an earthquake and all the prison doors were opened; everyone's chains were loosed. Not only did God break them out of that situation, the jailer witnessing all of this inquired of David, what he needed to do to be saved. A two-fold breakthrough took place.

There is no situation or problem too hard for God. The word of God says,

"Then the word of the LORD came to Jeremiah: [27] "I am the LORD, the God of all mankind. Is anything too hard for me? (Jeremiah 32:26-27)

We serve a God who cannot fail; a God that has ALL power in His hands; A God that can move mountains and calm raging seas. We serve a God that can speak to the wind and it submits in obedience; who can call the dead from the grave; that restores sight to the blind; speech to the mute and hearing to the deaf. What a mighty God we serve! So during your storms and torrential rains; when you're in the heat of the fire; realize that God is right there with you waiting to break you out and bring you through.

PRAYER OF EMPOWERMENT:

Father, I thank you for the realization that you are the God of the break-out and breakthrough. I know that there is nothing too hard for you. Thank you for showing me that there is no situation, no problem that you are unable to solve; for in you all things are possible. Father, strengthen me along life's journey to continue to trust and believe in you completely. I believe your word and I stand on your promises. Father, I praise you for being the God of the breakout. Amen

WHEN MORNING COMES…..

SCRIPTURAL EMPHASIS:

Psalms 30:5 - For his anger [endureth but] a moment; in his favour [is] life: weeping may endure for a night, but joy [cometh] in the morning.

Are the circumstances of life overwhelming you? Are you facing economic hardships? Is everything around you seemingly falling apart? Are you facing surmountable attacks from the enemy? Well, I have good news for you…It's only temporary.

It is refreshing to know that the trials and struggles in life that a Christian endures are only temporary. We have a constant hope that what we face on today will soon be a distant memory and an ultimate testimony of victory. We need not fret over what we see, because we walk by faith and not by sight. We have to look beyond what our natural eyes see, to catch a glimpse of what our spiritual eyes have captured about our future.

The Word of God says in Romans 8:18, *For I reckon that the sufferings of this present time are not worthy to be compared with the glory which shall be revealed in us.*

Going deeper inside of this scripture we find that, what we go through now cannot compare to the awesome glory of what God

is going to do on our behalf and what He's going to release in us. We should live with joyful anticipation that better days are ahead.

I'm reminded of a great songwriter Timothy Wright who penned the song, "Trouble Don't Last Always". The song goes on to say, He may not come when you want Him, but He's right on time….In times of trouble, He's a friend of mine, When storm clouds rise in your life, He'll be there, All your burdens, He will bear….I'm so glad…trouble don't last always. The song goes on to say as it does in Psalms 30:5, that weeping may endure for a night, but joy will come in the morning.

How powerful it is to know that the trials and struggles of life…are only but for a moment, because when morning comes….JOY! Sweet joy will be found. When the sea of life becomes temperamental and the winds began to fiercely blow, just know that God is in the midst of the storm and as long as we keep our eyes steadfast on Him, He will say to the wind and the waves, "Peace be still".

At the end of our tests and trials victory will always prevail. Your misery will turn into ministry. Your test will become your testimony. Your pain will become your passion. Your grief will become your glory. Your affliction will become your anointing. Your tragedies will become your triumphs.

The word of God says in Lamentations 3:18,

[18]And I said, My strength and my hope is perished from the LORD: [19]Remembering mine affliction and my misery, the wormwood and the gall. [20]My soul hath them still in remembrance, and is humbled in me. [21]This I recall to my mind, therefore have I hope. [22]It is of the LORD's mercies that we are not consumed, because his compassions fail not. [23]They are new every morning: great is thy faithfulness.

[24]The LORD is my portion saith my soul; therefore will I hope in him.

How you respond to your test and trials determine how you will go through and come out of them. If you complain, murmur and bicker, your testing will become very taxing on you. It will cause stress and depression, despair and sadness, tears and sorrow. But if you do as James 1: 2 states (My brethren, count it all joy when you fall into various trials) you will find that what you're going through will become increasingly more insignificant as you praise your way through it. As you're praising your way through the storm and the trying of your faith something wonderful transpires. James 1:3-4 goes on to say, *knowing that the testing of your faith produces patience. [4] But let patience have its perfect work, that you may be perfect and complete, lacking nothing.*

So you mean to tell me as I go through responding to my test and trials with praise that my faith will produce a positive harvest called patience? And if I allow patience to have its perfect work in me that I will become mature and well developed…not deficient in anything? What a wonderful reward for enduring tests and trials!

So when you feel like the cares of life are choking you to death, just know that it's only temporary. God is still and will always be in control. Test and trials come to make us strong. The more we respond in faith, the stronger we become. Don't give up, don't throw in the towel, and don't cave in for the breaking of day is just ahead. The sun will shine again.

The word hope in the Hebrew translation – Tohelet – means expectation. It is derived from the root yāḥal which means to wait, to be patient, cause to have or make to have hope, to stay, tarry, and trust, to be in pain. The Apostle Paul was afflicted with thorns in his side, he prayed three times to God for healing, but God responded this way in 2 Corinthians 12:9, My Grace is sufficient for thee; for my strength is made perfect in weakness. God could have just honored his request by immediately healing him, but a greater lesson was to be gleaned. It wasn't necessary to remove what only required the sufficient grace of God to aid in enduring the discomfort. Sometimes the limp that we may be left with will keep us grounded. The limp that is a result of the test and trials that we face reminds us that even in weakness I am strong only through the power and grace of God.

It reminds us that our strength is limited, but the strength of God is limitless. It reminds us that our faith and total dependence should be completely in God. The Message version of 2 Corinthians 12:7-10 makes it crystal clear.

7-10Because of the extravagance of those revelations, and so I wouldn't get a big head, I was given the gift of a handicap to keep me in constant touch with my limitations. Satan's angel did his best to get me down; what he in fact did was push me to my knees. No danger then of walking around high and mighty! At first I didn't think of it as a gift, and begged God to remove it. Three times I did that, and then he told me, my grace is enough; it's all you need. My strength comes into its own in your weakness. Once I heard that, I was glad to let it happen. I quit focusing on the handicap and began appreciating the gift. It was a case of Christ's strength moving in on my weakness. Now I take limitations in stride, and with good cheer, these limitations that cut me down to size—abuse, accidents, opposition, bad breaks. I just let Christ take over! And so the weaker I get, the stronger I become.

Could this be true? The weaker I become when I go thru the trials of life the stronger I become? Absolutely! Because our strength is not based on our physical stature, but on the contrary it is based on our powerful God. We must learn to be content in whatever state we are found in. Philippians 4:12 says in the Amplified version,

I know how to be abased and live humbly in straitened circumstances, and I know also how to enjoy plenty and live in abundance. I have learned in any and all circumstances the secret of facing every situation, whether well-fed or going hungry, having a sufficiency and enough to spare or going without and being in want.

When test and trials come, rejoice and know that it's only for a moment. When morning comes, weeping will cease and joy will increase. When morning comes, weakness will turn into strength. When morning comes, lack will turn into overflow and abundance. The discomfort of your night season will soon be replaced by the comfort of morning. When the night season completes its cycle, it cannot hold back the imminent force of daybreak. So don't fret in your night season, don't retreat in your night season, don't give up in your night season; "Morning is coming".

PRAYER OF EMPOWERMENT:

Father, thank you for showing me that trouble won't last always. Thank you for strengthening me to stand firm on your word in the midst of my test and trials. Thank you for showing me that your grace is sufficient and that your strength is made perfect in weakness. Father, forgive me for murmuring and complaining when instead I should praise you in the midst of the storm. Thank you for the thorns, because they remind me of my limitless strength and the need to be totally dependent upon you. Teach me to be content in whatever state I'm in, and to never take anything for granted. Thank you for the night seasons....for while I'm yet in the night season I have great anticipation that when morning comes, joy will greet me.

Amen

PEARLS OF WISDOM & GUIDANCE

"PROTECT YOUR PEARLS"

SCRIPTURAL EMPHASIS:

"Don't waste what is holy on people who are unholy. Don't throw your pearls to pigs! They will trample the pearls, then turn and attack you. (Matthew 7:6 NLT)

The Disciples were cautioned not to waste what is holy on the unholy. The holy teachings and instructions of Christ were to remain sacred. It is futile to pour into the life of someone who does not desire to know Christ intimately. They will only reject what is being said to them and then take truth and twist and distort it into something wicked and deceptive.

It is abundantly clear that the pig or swine is one of the filthiest animals ever. It has been argued that the pig is not fit to be sacrificed or consumed as food. A pig will play in the mud then clean itself up just to jump right back into the mud. If we take a look at this in the spiritual sense we can attest that there are those who continually jump in and out of the ring of sin. One day they're on fire for God the next day they are defiling and desecrating their temples with all kinds of filth. A part of them desires to be clean; but the other part of them can't rid their desire to play in the cesspool of sin. They allow themselves to be entangled in the very thing they once were freed from. In essence they've become a slave to sin.

They brag about themselves with empty, foolish boasting. With an appeal to twisted sexual desires, they lure back into sin those who have barely escaped from a lifestyle of deception. [19] They promise freedom, but they themselves are slaves of sin and corruption. For you are a slave to whatever controls you. [20] And when people escape from the wickedness of the world by knowing our Lord and Savior Jesus Christ and then get tangled up and enslaved by sin again, they are worse off than before. [21] It would be better if they had never known the way to righteousness than to know it and then reject the command they were given to live a holy life. [22] They prove the truth of this proverb: "A dog returns to its vomit."[a] And another says, "A washed pig returns to the mud." (2 Peter 2:18-22 NLT)

Don't waste your pearls on these people! Yes, we are to reach the lost at any cost, but when a person continues to wallow in sin, we must remove ourselves and place them in the hands of the Lord. They don't deserve to partake of your pearls. They in essence are making a mockery out of you and the word you impart to them. They're wasting your time and effort. They would rather reject the truth to believe and live a lie. These people have no respect for God or you. At this point, it is time to disengage. We must be very careful who we give our pearls to. There are those who simply put, despise truth and will reject wisdom and godly counsel.

The fear of the LORD is the beginning of knowledge; fools despise wisdom and instruction. (Proverbs 1:7 ESV)

Speak not in the ears of a fool: for he will despise the wisdom of thy words. (Proverbs 23:9 KJV)

The bible teaches us that a time will come when there will be many who will not take heed to sound doctrine. They will seek out weak and watered down messages. They will seek out a feel good tickle my fancy word. They will seek out "have it your way" messages. They will reject the truth.

For the time will come when they will not endure sound doctrine; but after their own lusts shall they heap to themselves teachers, having itching ears; (2 Timothy 4:3 KJV)

We are to present and offer the word of God in love to those who do not know Christ in the pardon of their sins; not standing in a judgmental posture; but we are to offer the word of God in all humility and long-suffering. It is not for us to judge the validity of their confession, but if they reject our offering we then cannot force them to receive it. Instead we must disengage and continue to pray that their eyes and hearts will be opened to receive the truth. We simply cannot force the truth of God's word on anyone. God is a gentleman. He never forces Himself on anyone. He beckons us to hear and yield to His call; it is then up to us to repent and receive.

It is imperative that we recognize those who are truly receptive from those who have no desire to receive and from those who know the word of truth but desire only to be controlled and enslaved by the pleasure of sin. A person who truly desires change will do whatever it takes to change. Those who know the truth and refuse the truth great will be their consequence. I'm reminded of an old saying, "you can lead a horse to the water, but you can't make it drink".

We must be very careful that as we are trying to draw others to Christ that we do not become judgmental. We must remember that we all were once sinners and in bondage. We must know what to say, how to say it and when to say it. Our approach must always be founded on and delivered in love.

But speaking the truth in love may grow up into him in all things, which is the head, even Christ: (Ephesians 4:15 KJV)

We must examine our intent and motives; ensuring that we are not operating with hidden agendas and selfish gratification. We must not appear pompous or arrogant; as if we are perfect creatures. The bible tells us that we have all sinned and fallen short. We do not want to appear self righteous or condescending. Our position is meant to build up not tear down. We must not allow the rejection of the word by others frustrate or aggravate us, but we must realize we must always be wise when we attempt to win souls. Our response must always be saturated in the love of God. We will encounter those whose hearts are hardened, but we must tread lightly and speak from the wise counsel of the word of God.

Behold, I send you forth as sheep in the midst of wolves: be ye therefore wise as serpents, and harmless as doves. (Matthew 10:16 KJV)

The Sovereign LORD has given me his words of wisdom, so that I know how to comfort the weary.
Morning by morning he wakens me and opens my understanding to his will. (Isaiah 50:4 NLT)

Do not be dismayed when you have shared the word of God to others in hopes that they might accept Him as their Lord and Savior and they decide to reject the truth. You've done what you were commissioned to do. All you can do is continue in prayer for that individual that they may have a change of heart and mind and come into the knowledge of Christ before it's too late.

PRAYER OF EMPOWERMENT:

Father, I thank you for the power of your word and the gospel message of hope and salvation. Empower me to continue to seek the lost; that they may repent and accept you as their Lord and Savior. Equip me with the words of knowledge and wisdom to speak words of life, hope and encouragement to the lost. Help me not to stand in judgment of others; realizing that I too was once a sinner enslaved to sin. Let my life be an example of your love and saving grace. Empower me to speak with the tongue of the learned; that I may know how to speak a word in season to the lost and weary. Amen

WHO'S TOUCHING YOU

SCRIPTURAL EMPHASIS:

Lay hands suddenly on no man, neither be partaker of other men's sins: keep thyself pure. I Timothy 5:22

We must be very mindful of who we allow to touch us spiritually and naturally. One wrong touch could devastate and destroy your entire life. Who we allow in our inner circle is very important and vital to our successes and or failures. If we allow the wrong person to get too close to us we can and will forfeit our blessed promise. Even so, we must also be careful of those who serve alongside of us. Some people in church are merely there on assignment to steal your blessings, destroy your destiny, and kill your existence; wolves in sheep clothing.

It is also crucially important to be wise in who you allow to speak into your ear. Avoid soliciting the carnal opinions of others concerning your issues. Some people will only tell you what you want to hear. They will not offer sound biblical counsel, but instead they will sugarcoat and pacify you. These people do not have your best interest at heart. Be assured, they have a hidden agenda and hidden motives. You should only involve yourself with those who only desire to see you succeed and those who will push you to the next level. Those who will pray with you and for you; standing in the gap on your behalf so that your destiny will be made manifest. You should only seek Kingdom minded people; those that will help you pursue your purpose.

In order to avoid succumbing to the wrong touch, you must be able to discern the voice of God. Avoid those that only desire to stroke your ego, but never is able to offer constructive criticism and correction. In 1 Samuel 3 we find the story of Samuel and Eli. Samuel was Eli's assistant. Eli was elderly and his vision had become dim. One night Eli had gone to bed and Samuel was asleep in the Tabernacle. The Lord called out to Samuel, but Samuel thought it was Eli calling him. Eli responds by telling Samuel to return to bed because he did not call him. Then the Lord called out again to Samuel; again Samuel went in to inquire of Eli if he called him. Again, Eli responded return to bed for I have not called you. Samuel did not yet know the Lord because he never heard the Lord speak to him before. His ear was not yet tuned to the voice of God. Once more the Lord called out to Samuel and once more he went in to inquire of Eli. At that moment Eli realized it was the Lord calling Samuel; he commanded Samuel to go back to bed and if he heard someone calling him again his response should be, "speak Lord, your servant is listening". The Lord again called out to Samuel a final time; this time Samuel replied, "Speak Lord, your servant is listening. We must know the voice of our Lord and Savior and when he beckons us we must answer, "Speak Lord, your servant is listening". Samuel kept answering flesh when it was the spirit calling him.

It's imperative that we not allow the wrong voice in our ear. Stop running to flesh for a spiritual answer. The wrong voice in our ears will attempt to distort and drown out the voice of the Lord. If we continue to solicit the voice of others, we won't be able to discern clearly when God is speaking to us.

Listening to the wrong people will cause you to miss vital instructions from God. In Joshua 1 we find that Moses the servant of God is now dead. The Lord speaks to Joshua to charging him to lead the Israelites across the Jordan River into the land He prepared for them. Joshua's ability to hear the voice of God allowed him to walk in authority; carrying out the charge of the Lord.

Please note that sometimes your plans and desires may not end the way you designed them to end. You will face opposition, pressure and pain. It is in this phase that we must not lose our focus. Do not allow negative words to be spoken from your lips. There will be people on assignment that will come trying to knock you off course. They will try and get you to give up on what God has ordained you to do. In this arena be sure not to succumb to negative people. Do not allow negative comments to distract you and cause you to doubt. Your faith must be activated and in full operation. Remember the trying of your faith develops patience. (James 1:3) Do not become slack or lazy during this time. Hebrews 6:12 NLT states, Then you will not become spiritually dull and indifferent. Instead, you will follow the example of those who are going to inherit God's promises because of their faith and endurance.

Dismiss all who come to deter you from the promise. No matter how hard your test and trials become. No matter the losses you may incur; stay focused on the Lord. Job was the epitome of suffering and loss. He loss everything he had. His health was afflicted. His friends disserted him. Yet he stood steadfast in his faith in God. His wife even tried to persuade him to curse God and die. Instead Job remained vigilant in faith. His trust in God was unwavering. He wasn't sure how God or if God was going to bring him out but he knew that his only hope was in God. Sometimes you have to stand alone. You may just have to lose it all to gain it all.

When you stand in faith, God will send someone along your path to encourage you and build you up. This kingdom minded individual will be driven to reveal the treasure that lives within you. God will send a word of hope that your latter days shall be greater and the best is yet to come. Continue striving for spiritual excellence. If you continue to be faithful over the little, God will bless you to be ruler over many. Your destiny is within reach. All those who rise up to deter you; God will take care of. He will, simply put; make your enemies your footstool. The very one that attempts to keep you down will be the one used to elevate you. Daily guard your heart and your mind. Let no evil communication be released from your lips. Therefore my beloved brothers, be ye steadfast, unmovable, always abounding in the work of the Lord, forasmuch as ye know, that your labor is not in vain in the Lord. (1 Corinthians 15:58)

PRAYER OF EMPOWERMENT:

Father God, empower me to dismiss all negative influences from my life. Empower me to discern those who have my best interest and those who are merely adorned in sheep clothing but are savage wolves seeking to destroy my destiny. Let me activate my faith when I'm faced with test and trials and when you re-route my course. Help me to stay focused on you. Let my feet follow the path you've designed for me. Father I pray that when the pressures of life are honing in on me; that I will rise up and stand on your word. Father I put my complete and total trust in you. I will remain steadfast and unmovable always abounding in the work of the Lord. Lord, I accept that if I suffer loss, in the end I'll gain everything.

Amen

"DON'T TOUCH THAT"

SCRIPTURE EMPHASIS:

Can a man take fire in his bosom and his clothes not be burned? (Proverbs 6:27 Amplified)

The Bible tells us in James 4:7, "Submit yourselves, then, to God. Resist the devil, and he will flee from you." This scripture should be etched in our hearts and minds as we walk with Christ. God is telling us we do not have to yield to our flesh...all we have to do is recognize that the enemy is plotting against us at all times and be ready to stand firm and tell the devil no.

I know some will say, "My flesh is just so weak". Well the Bible tells us that our flesh is weak. That's no big surprise, but he also tells us the spirit is willing. (Matthew 26:41b – NIV) The problem is that we depend more on the flesh than we do the spirit. We can't say that we are unable to overcome the flesh and its sinful desires, because Christ came in the form of flesh, yet he knew no sin. If we serve this same Christ, then we too can abstain from evil. It just requires us to allow the spirit complete operating control in our lives.

Do you remember when you were growing up as a young child your mother saying to you "Don't touch that, it's hot?" We've all gone through that phase in life. It's called I hear you but I'm going to do it anyway. Our curiosity overtakes us and we do exactly what we were told not to do only to find out what we were told was vital to us not being hurt or burned. Playing with fire will always result in getting burned.

Sin is no different. God is telling us today, "Don't touch that!" The Bible clearly teaches about not yielding to temptation. It instructs us that temptation is not of God nor does it come from God. Let's delve into this a little deeper.

James 1:13-15 tell us in the NIV text, *[13]When tempted, no one should say, "God is tempting me." For God cannot be tempted by evil, nor does he tempt anyone; [14]but each one is tempted when, by his own evil desire, he is dragged away and enticed. [15]Then, after desire has conceived, it gives birth to sin; and sin, when it is full-grown, gives birth to death.*

Clearly we can see here that God is not the author of temptation nor can He be tempted by evil. What actually takes place my friend is when our desires begin to entice us…that thought that drops in our head that begins to nibble at our strength and integrity…we get swept away by those thoughts. The more we think about it, the stronger the desire becomes and before you know it, your thought has now turned into action. The thing you conceived in your mind has now impregnated you, and what you give birth to is sin. That sin if not cut off, then grows and enlarges, and when it has fully taken over it produces death. The desires of our flesh are temporary and once we've acted on our desire we're left lifeless and guilt ridden.

But there is a way of escape! The Bible tells us in 1 Corinthians 10:13 NIV, *No temptation has seized you except what is common to man. And God is faithful; he will not let you be tempted beyond what you can bear. But when you are tempted, he will also provide a way out so that you can stand up under it.*

Isn't this encouraging news? Yes, we will absolutely be tempted, but the faithfulness of God will not allow us to be tempted beyond what we can handle. The temptation will come but the escape route is also provided. I love the Message translation of this very scripture, No test or temptation that comes your way is beyond the course of what others have had to face. All you need to remember is that God will never let you down; he'll never let you be pushed past your limit; he'll always be there to help you come through it. What a powerful word!

We can overcome sin! You must put your flesh on a diet....stop feeding it the wrong stuff. Be careful what you watch on television and in movies. Be careful what you allow your ears to listen to. Be careful of the company you keep and the conversations you involve yourselves in. Start feeding your spirit man that it might gain strength to overcome the enemy. Douse yourself in the word of God. Saturate your lives with prayer. Renew your spirit with praise and worship. You can overcome sin! The Bible says we are more than conquerors. Walk in that! Stop letting your flesh dictate to you your actions. When you plant the word in your life...you will produce the results of the Word. What you put in, is what you'll get out.

We must perfect Holiness. We must be holy as God commanded because He is holy. 2 Corinthians 7:1 KJV says, *having therefore these promises, dearly beloved, let us cleanse ourselves from all filthiness of the flesh and spirit, perfecting holiness in the fear of God.*

Holiness is not a tradition...it's a way of life. You belong to God. Your body belongs to God. Your mind belongs to God. 1 Corinthians 6:19 asks a question, *"What? Know ye not that your body is the temple of the Holy Ghost which is in you, which ye have of God, and ye are not your own?*

We don't belong to ourselves; we belong to God. So let us practice self control. Resist temptation and the lusts of this flesh. Walk in the spirit and after the things of the spirit. Denying your flesh may not feel good, but it's for your good!

PRAYER OF EMPOWERMENT:

Father, forgive me for yielding my flesh to the enemy. Strengthen me to embrace holiness as a way of life and not mere tradition as men see it. Teach me to delight myself in your laws and to follow only after the things of the spirit. Father, I know temptation will come, but I thank you for the escape route in advance. Teach me to practice only the things that will glorify and honor you. Let my life be exemplified by the fruits of the spirit. Amen

Human Nature VS Divine Instruction

"Don't Look Back"

SCRIPTURAL EMPHASIS: Genesis 19:17

And it came to pass, when they had brought them forth abroad, that he said, Escape for thy life; look not behind thee, neither stay thou in all the plain; escape to the mountain, lest thou be consumed.

Here we see the Lord giving "divine instruction" to Lot to run for his life. He's further instructed to not look back or stop moving but to escape into the mountains to avoid being consumed.

We can assess from this passage that it was direly important that Lot and his family remain focused on what was in front of them and to flee from what was behind them, because where they were would only lead to death, but where they were going life would be found.

Lot was in a place that was about to be completely destroyed. So it was absolutely necessary for him to uproot and move in order not to be consumed by the pending destruction of Sodom. Angels in disguise came to Lot to lead him and his family out of Sodom and out of harm's way. We must note that when you have to escape the way Lot and his family did it means you must leave friends, family, and possessions behind. It was imperative that Lot and his family left immediately because God was about to destroy Sodom and Gomorrah. They didn't have time to pack up their belongings. There wasn't a U-Haul rental truck to move their belongings. They had to take what they could and get out fast before they too were destroyed in the city.

God's divine instruction would lead them to safety, but as we all know some times human nature gets in the way and knocks us off course. Instead of following the instruction God had given to not look back....Lot's wife looked back and was turned into a pillar of salt.

She was unable to detach herself from what was comfortable and familiar to trust the instruction of God that would take her to a place of safety and yield her a new life.

Today we bear the same struggle. God is telling us to keep pressing forward. He's warning us not to look back because what's behind us will lead to death, but what's before us will lead to abundant life.

Let's take a look at a few things God warns us to flee from. Flee means to run away often from danger or evil; to hurry toward a place of security.

In 1 Corinthians 6:18 the Word of God tells us to:

Flee fornication; every sin that a man doeth is without the body; but he that committeth fornication sinneth against his own body.

Let's break this down and take a look at what the "Message" version says about 1 Corinthians 6:18:

There's more to sex than mere skin on skin. Sex is as much spiritual mystery as physical fact. As written in Scripture, "The two become one." Since we want to become spiritually one with the Master, we must not pursue the kind of sex that avoids commitment and intimacy, leaving us lonelier than ever—the kind of sex that can never "become one." There is a sense in which sexual sins are different from all others. In sexual sin we violate the sacredness of our own bodies, these bodies that were made for God-given and God-modeled love, for "becoming one" with another. Or didn't you realize that your body is a sacred place, the place of the Holy Spirit? Don't you see that you can't live however you please; squandering what God paid such a high price for? The physical part of you is not some piece of property belonging to the spiritual part of you. God owns the whole works. So let people see God in and through your body.

Next let's take a look at 1 Corinthians 10:14:

Wherefore, my dearly beloved, flee from idolatry.

This simply put means when you see people reducing God to something they can use or control, get out of their company as fast as you can.

I want to take a look at one more thing (there are many more) that God warns us to flee from.

2 Timothy 2:22 says, *Flee also youthful lusts: but follow righteousness, faith, charity, peace, with them that call on the Lord out of a pure heart.*

I also like the breakdown of the Message version of this scripture;

Run away from infantile indulgence. Run after mature righteousness—faith, love, peace joining those who are in honest and serious prayer before God. Refuse to get involved in inane discussions; they always end up in fights. God's servant must not be argumentative, but a gentle listener and a teacher who keeps cool, working firmly but patiently with those who refuse to obey. You never know how or when God might sober them up with a change of heart and a turning to the truth, enabling them to escape the Devil's trap, where they are caught and held captive, forced to run his errands.

God warns His people to flee from evil things and it's up to us to obey his "Divine Instruction" and not yield to our own human nature; remembering that doing things our way leads to death but being led by the Spirit leads to and produces life.

Meditate on this scripture:

Philippians 3:13-14: *Brethren, I count not myself to have apprehended: but this one thing I do, forgetting those things which are behind, and reaching forth unto those things which are before, I press toward the mark for the prize of the high calling of God in Christ Jesus.*

Don't look back because a backward glance will lead to a lost promise.

PRAYER OF EMPOWERMENT:

Father, empower me to always follow your instructions. Lead and guide me down the path of life that you've chosen for me. Order my steps and make my way plain. Father, I have not attained all there is to attain, but I've decided to forget what is behind me and reach for what is before me. Father, strengthen me to keep my eyes fixed on you. Lord, remove every hindrance and attachment that is not like you. Lord, I will continue to press forward and pursue the promise. Amen

SHH....

SCRIPTURAL EMPHASIS:

James 1:19 - Wherefore, my beloved brethren, let every man be swift to hear, slow to speak, slow to wrath:

During a period of fasting and consecration, I found myself not wanting to do much talking. While sitting at my desk at work one day, I began to think about how quiet I had been. I'm sure some may have thought I was being anti-social and introverted. Then God spoke to me in the stillness of the moment and said Shh! Listen!

Sometimes we get so caught up in yesterday's news, and today's drama that we spend countless hours talking about things that bear no importance, things that are futile in nature, and more importantly things that do not glorify and/or edify God. It's amazing to me that when you steal away into a place of solace that you begin to realize that a lot of conversations we have are senseless. We are all guilty of just plain ole talking too much. We have to instead drift away into that calm, quiet, and peaceful place that requires no talking unless we're talking to God.

I too am guilty of talking too much, and I had to repent of that very thing. Sometimes although it's rude to say, we all need to just shut up and listen. Some would inquire, "Listen to what?" Listen for the voice of God. Please note that you may not always receive an audible message from God, but in the stillness of the moment God is speaking. He's speaking to your heart and your mind. He's whispering sweet something's in your ear. He's interceding on your behalf. He's speaking to the car that is about to run your car off the road. He's speaking to the hurricane force winds that's about to blow the roof off of your home. Just because you may not hear him, doesn't mean he's not speaking.

I remember when I was a little girl and it would begin to storm outside, my Mother would say "OK, get somewhere and sit down, be still and be quiet." She would say, "Pray". She believed that in the midst of the storm, it wasn't time for everyone to be rambunctious and loud, but it was time for everyone to quiet themselves and be still, while God was attending to His work. I learned early that even in the midst of a storm, God is speaking.

Mark 4:36-39 proves this statement:
[36]And when they had sent away the multitude, they took him even as he was in the ship. And there were also with him other little ships. [37]And there arose a great storm of wind, and the waves beat into the ship, so that it was now full. [38]And he was in the hinder part of the ship, asleep on a pillow: and they awake him, and say unto him, Master, carest thou not that we perish? [39]And he arose, and rebuked the wind, and said unto the sea, Peace, be still. And the wind ceased, and there was a great calm.

In the midst of the storm, keep your resolve. Don't allow the storm to cause you to fear or doubt. Trust in God completely, knowing that He will deliver you out of the storm. Sometimes when you're in a storm it requires you to be still and quiet so that you can hear the voice of God clearly. When there's a lot of noise and commotion you can miss what God is trying to say.

We as people in general have a tendency of talking way too much. Then we get upset and angry when we don't receive a response or the response we expected to receive. Well, that's the problem. We get so caught up in getting our point across or fighting and defending our cause that we don't leave space for response. God is trying to convey the answer to us but we cut Him off mid sentence. One thing about God is He is a gentleman.

He won't try and out speak you or talk over you. He waits patiently for his turn to respond. If you're always speaking and never listening, God can't respond to your dilemma. Your deliverance is waiting on you to be quiet long enough to hear the voice of God.

God is not the author of confusion. When everyone is talking at the same time, it breeds confusion. If you can just be still and hold your peace, the Bible says the Lord will fight your battle. No matter what you're facing, tell God about it and then wait patiently with your ears tuned for His response. His response may not be audible, but it may very well be revealed through the scriptures. Reading and studying the word of God is the best way to tune your ears to hear the voice of God. It is much more difficult to be quiet before the Lord and listen for his voice than actually speaking to God. The Bible tells us to be slow to speak but quick to listen. (James 1:19) We should cultivate the art of being silent.

Psalms 62:1 (KJV) states, *"Truly my soul waiteth upon God: from Him my cometh my salvation.*

When you wait upon the Lord; God will renew your strength. The Bible tells us if we wait patiently on Him; He will hear our cry. But if we are loud and boisterous we are stifling the hand of God to move on our behalf. God doesn't react or respond to your rants and raves. He'll sit quietly until you come to Him in humility and complete submission. When we petition God we must wait patiently for His response. Don't expect God to move when you want Him to move. His timing is not our timing. But one thing is for sure, God will respond to your situation, but will you be able to identify His voice when he responds? Will you maintain your silence long enough to hear from God? Will you cease from speaking and allow God to answer? If you can't make time to listen to God; you will never hear God speak.

PRAYER OF EMPOWERMENT:

Father, forgive me for talking too much. Teach me how to sit in silence, patiently waiting to hear from you. I realize that communication is about speaking and listening. Teach me to know when to speak and when to remain quiet. Lord, when I pray teach me to sit in peace so that I may hear your response. Forgive me for every time I've ranted and raved, trying to move you to respond. Lord I yield my life to you and I desire to know and hear your voice clearly. Thank you for prayers heard and answered. Let me not utter one word out of due season. Let the words of my mouth and the meditation of my heart; be acceptable in thy sight, O Lord, my strength and my redeemer.

Amen

LET IT GO

SCRIPTURAL EMPHASIS:

Colossians 3:1-10 (NIV) - [1]Since, then, you have been raised with Christ, set your hearts on things above, where Christ is seated at the right hand of God. [2]Set your minds on things above, not on earthly things. [3]For you died and your life is now hidden with Christ in God. [4]When Christ, who is your life, appears, then you also will appear with him in glory. [5]Put to death, therefore, whatever belongs to your earthly nature: sexual immorality, impurity, lust, evil desires and greed, which is idolatry. [6]Because of these, the wrath of God is coming. [7]You used to walk in these ways, in the life you once lived. [8]But now you must rid yourselves of all such things as these: anger, rage, malice, slander, and filthy language from your lips. [9]Do not lie to each other, since you have taken off your old self with its practices [10]and have put on the new self, which is being renewed in knowledge in the image of its Creator.

It's time to "LET IT ALL GO". Warning comes before destruction. So it's imperative that we obey the voice of God and do as He has commanded us to do. Be mindful of who you are, who you belong to and who you serve. If you're a servant of Christ then you should look, act, talk, walk, and be just like Him. Your conversation should be Holy. Your thoughts should be Holy thoughts. There should be nothing about us that is contrary to our confession of Christ. I admonish you to stop

saying what you're not going to do and just don't do it. Every time you say you're not going to smoke, drink, fornicate, gossip, lie, steal, cheat, listen to secular music or watch ungodly things…God is recording it in the book. And each time you renege and do what you say you're not going to do…God is recording it in the book. Each time you go back and forth it represents instability. It represents to God that you can't be trusted and that you're double minded. It represents that you don't trust God enough to replace what you thought you needed, with what you truly need to survive. It represents a lack of character and integrity. So the next time you have a negative urge to do something outside the perfect will of God; remember that it's being recorded….our every thoughts are being recorded. We can't escape the intellect and knowledge of Christ. He's ever present, and all knowing. So those things we do in secret…He knows before the thought is even formed in our minds. It's time for everyone to choose today who you're going to serve. Serving two masters is not an option…either you love God and hate satan or you love satan and hate God.

We need to get serious about God. He's the one and only true and living God. The one, who hung, bled and died on Calvary's cross for our filth and shame. It's time to pay our respect to our Lord and Savior every day for the rest of our lives; by offering our lives to Christ as a living sacrifice; standing humble before the King of Kings and the Lord of Lords with a willing and a open heart; available for His use and His use only.

We can fool each other; slip, slide, duck and hide; but we will never fool God because He knows every intimate thought; he knows our every flaw and frailty. He knows what we're going to do before we do it. We must get real and stay real with God; before he exposes every nook and cranny of our so called private lives. God is about to do random strip searches and expose every demonic and foul thought and action that has been kept hidden in the shadows of life and bring them to the fore-front for all to see. Again, warning comes before destruction. I'm taking heed and if it's not like God…it's got to go. If it doesn't please God….it won't please me. Our pleasure is to take delight in the awesome wonder of God; to serve him with gladness; with a spirit of humility and love. It's preparation time. We must live today as if He's coming back tomorrow.

It's time to give it all up. Everything that's not like God; everything that is not pleasing to God; Everything that does not line up with the word of God…every foul, perverse and demonic influence…every foul and perverse thought and/or characteristic. Our DNA has to link to Christ. If we belong to Christ, our test results should read; "God is your Father." So let us be forever mindful of who we serve; who we belong to; and who we represent. Let's do a self check right now; "Is my life a good representation of Christ?" "Can my peers and co-workers see Christ in me or do I blend in to fit in?" "Is my life conformed to Christ or to the world?" "Would I have this conversation with God?" Every day all throughout the day we need to do a self check. It is far better for us to evaluate and check ourselves than to continue in sin and have God check us.

We must be real and radical about Christ. We must represent our Father so that those around us that may not know Him or that have strayed from Him will come to know Him in the pardon of their sins. We are the light of the world…if we hide our light…if we blend in to fit in with the world…who are we helping? It's time to get right, stay right or be left.

PRAYER OF EMPOWERMENT:

Father, forgive us for holding onto things that is not profitable to our lives and our walk with you. Father, forgive us for saying one thing and doing another. Forgive us for trying to serve two masters. Lord, help us to live everyday as if tomorrow you would return. Teach us to trust in your word and to obey your every command. Father, help us to let it all go, to take up our cross and follow you completely. Strengthen us today Lord, that we may represent you in all that we say and do; that we will be found worthy of the vocation whereby we have been called. Amen

PEARLS OF ENLIGHTENMENT

REFLECTIONS

SCRIPTURAL EMPHASIS:

John 3:1-2 (Amplified Bible)

[1]SEE WHAT [[a]an incredible] quality of love the Father has given (shown, bestowed on) us, that we should [be permitted to] be named and called and counted the children of God! And so we are! The reason that the world does not know (recognize, acknowledge) us is that it does not know (recognize, acknowledge) Him.

[2]Beloved, we are [even here and] now God's children; it is not yet disclosed (made clear) what we shall be [hereafter], but we know that when He comes and is manifested, we shall [[b]as God's children] resemble and be like Him, for we shall see Him [c]just as He [really] is.

Today I want us to reflect on the beauty of God and His entire majestic splendor. We have so much to be thankful to God for. As I was sitting here contemplating what inspirational nugget I could deposit today, I heard the word, "REFLECTION". I want to look at two aspects of this word. The root word is reflect....to think quietly and calmly. Sometimes we must quiet ourselves long enough to sit back and just reflect on the goodness of Jesus, and in doing so we will see how beautiful and amazing God truly is. If we would just take five or ten minutes out of each day to close our eyes, clear our minds and reflect on where we were this time last year to where we are now…we would see God in a way that we've never seen Him before. This time last year you were headed for divorce, but God restored your marriage and now you're deeply in love and completely happy. You had no idea that what was considered to be dead; God would breathe new life into and resurrect a seemingly dead situation. This time last year your house was in foreclosure, but God stepped in and turned even that situation around and now you're about to purchase a second home. Just look at how good our God is. Look how far God has brought us. All glory belongs to God. So I challenge you to take 5 minutes out of every day to close our eyes, quiet ourselves and your surroundings and just "reflect" on the goodness of Jesus.

Now let's take a look at the complete word…"reflection"…..an effect produced by an influence. This definition in and of itself is powerful. An effect produced by an influence…..Just repeat this to yourself a few times…"An effect produced by an influence." God is our influence; the more intimate we become with God the more we reflect (to make manifest or apparent) His image. Have you ever looked at an older couple that's been married for sixty or seventy years and notice how much they look and act alike? They've been married for so long that they begin to talk alike, walk alike, and even eat alike. They both share the same qualities and characteristics because they've lived and communed together for years upon years. I would dare to believe that their hearts beat in unison. This is how it ought to be with us and our communion with God. We should spend so much time with God that we begin to mirror his image. Our lives should be a mirrored representation of Christ. When people look at us they should see Christ. This does not happen overnight but it will happen if we continue to put our focus on the Lord, commune with Him daily and stand in complete obedience to His every command.

We have been given the best instruction manual we will ever have in life and that's the Word of God. For within the word of God we find LIFE. It teaches us everything we need to live an abundant and victorious life. If you don't spend time with God you will never mirror the image of God. So ask yourself today, "Do I reflect (make manifest) the image of Christ?" The Word tells us that God is coming back for a church that is without spot, blemish or wrinkle. The only way to possess these attributes is to yield our lives to God completely and walk in complete obedience which produces a mirrored effect of the influence of Christ.

I pray this has inspired you to strive toward grooming your life to reflect the image of Christ.

PRAYER OF EMPOWERMENT:

Father, as I commune with you and become more intimate with you thru prayer, worship and the Word, let my image mirror your image. I pray when people see me that they see you. Father I pray that my life is a direct representation of your influence. Lord let my life be a direct expression of your life as I continue to walk in complete obedience to your word.

Amen

"BEYOND THE MASK"

SCRIPTURAL EMPHASIS:

[8] If we claim we have no sin, we are only fooling ourselves and not living in the truth. [9] But if we confess our sins to him, he is faithful and just to forgive us our sins and to cleanse us from all wickedness. [10] If we claim we have not sinned, we are calling God a liar and showing that his word has no place in our hearts. (1 John 1:8-10)

God imparted this topic to me I believe because he wants the people of God to move beyond the facades and remove the masks that cover who we really are. I'm reminded of a song written by India Arie, "I am not my hair; what a powerful and relevant song! It is a true and real statement. This external appearance is not who I am internally. The makeup I wear does not make me any less vulnerable. It just covers up my blemishes and enhances my God given natural beauty.

God declares in His word that the outward man is not His concern, but the inward man; the soul of a man; the heart of man is what he looks upon. He's not judging our looks but our hearts. Sometimes we are covering up what God is trying to reveal…we hide what God is trying to heal. God is looking for a people who will stand before Him naked and unashamed.

Man sees our flaws and faults but God sees the hearts intent, our purpose, our motives and our destiny. Underneath all the makeup and the masks we wear still lie the issues of life. When we get to the point where we can stand before God unmasked and uncovered, God will then be able to operate in us and through us. But instead we cover up our hurts and our pain with feeble attempts of turning up the corners of mouths to display a smile. We don't want anyone to see weakness in us. We don't want others to know we really don't have it all together.

We look like a million dollars on the outside, but on the inside we're crying out desperately for help. Because we're afraid to stand before God bare, we hold on to insecurities, low self esteem, with little or no confidence. We want to appear that we have it all together. We want to appear as a blossoming flower, but inwardly we're wilting and being choked out by the weeds of life.

All God is waiting on is for us to drop the facade; remove the mask; baring ourselves completely before him so that he can mend what's broken; heal what's hurting; and cast out that which torments us. What happens is instead of trusting God completely we put limits on God. We tie His hands. We speak negatively day in and day out. We deny that there's even a problem. But it's time to remove the mask. It's time to bare all before God. Plastic surgery isn't the answer. You're only altering the mask and not removing it.

The mask must be removed so you can stand surrendered before God in complete submission. It's imperative that we surrender to God; allowing the Master Surgeon to remove what's no longer needed, replacing it with that which will sustain, strengthen, and mature us.

Removing the mask requires one to be fearless because it will expose the real you. It will reveal the person that God wants to use. Removing the mask frees you from the bondage that was attached to the mask. When we remove our masks it attracts others to us. Our witness becomes more effective because others will see the real us. We become transparent so that others see God in us. Removing the mask is not just to benefit you but to be a witness to others.

I admonish you…people of God…Remove the mask; tear down the façade; stand before God naked and unashamed. Let the Lord mold you and make you. Let God cover you. When God covers you; you're covered and own the right to wear the crown and hold the title of being a child of God.

PRAYER OF EMPOWERMENT:

Father God, I've hidden who I am for far too long. I've covered up my faults, frailties, hurts, and pain. I've worn a mask so that others could not see the real me. Father, but I want to stand before you naked and unashamed. I want to stand before you in complete submission, and that requires me to remove what I've kept hidden and allow you to strengthen, heal, and restore me, so that I can be a witness and an example to others. Thank you for revealing the real me; strengthen me to continue to stand before you in complete surrender so that others will see you in me. Amen

GOT SUBSTANCE?

SCRIPTURAL EMPHASIS: Ephesians 4:11-16 (Amplified)

[11]And His gifts were [varied; He Himself appointed and gave men to us] some to be apostles (special messengers), some prophets (inspired preachers and expounders), some evangelists (preachers of the Gospel, traveling missionaries), some pastors (shepherds of His flock) and teachers. [12]His intention was the perfecting and the full equipping of the saints (His consecrated people), [that they should do] the work of ministering toward building up Christ's body (the church), [13][That it might develop] until we all attain oneness in the faith and in the comprehension of the [[a]full and accurate] knowledge of the Son of God, that [we might arrive] at really mature manhood (the completeness of personality which is nothing less than the standard height of Christ's own perfection), the measure of the stature of the fullness of the Christ and the completeness found in Him. [14]So then, we may no longer be children, tossed [like ships] to and fro between chance gusts of teaching and wavering with every changing wind of doctrine, [the prey of] the cunning and cleverness of [b]unscrupulous men, [gamblers engaged] in every shifting form of trickery in inventing errors to mislead. [15]Rather, let our lives lovingly [c]express truth [in all things, speaking truly, dealing truly, living truly]. Enfolded in love, let us grow up in every way and in all things into Him, who is the Head, [even] Christ (the Messiah, the Anointed One). [16]For because of Him the whole body (the church, in all its various parts), closely joined and firmly knit together by the joints and ligaments with which it is supplied, when each part [with power adapted to its need] is working properly [in all its functions], grows to full maturity, building itself up in love.

There are two words I'd like to look at; maturity and substance. You can't have one without the other. If there's no substance there's no maturity.

Webster's definition of maturity is "full development". The Greek translation of the word mature is Teleaos – meaning complete and perfect.

Maturity in Christ is essential. The word of God is designed to be our guide to living the way God ordained us to live. It provides sound principles to living a victorious life over sin. In order to mature in Christ we must study the word daily and put it into action in our daily lives. Maturity has nothing to do with age, gender, financial status, or race.

Maturity is not based upon designer labels, houses, cars, fine linen, or your gifts and talents. Maturity has nothing to do with your successes and achievements; nor does it involve your college degree.

Maturity involves a deeper understanding of the word of God. Hebrews 6:1 (Amp) states,

Therefore let us go on and get past the elementary stage in the teachings and doctrine of Christ (the Messiah), advancing steadily toward the completeness and perfection that belong to spiritual maturity. Let us not again be laying the foundation of repentance and abandonment of dead works (dead formalism) and of the faith [by which you turned] to God, ²With teachings about purifying, the laying on of hands, the resurrection from the dead, and eternal judgment and punishment. [These are all matters of which you should have been fully aware long, long ago.]

I love how the Message translation puts it. (Hebrews 6:1-3)

1-3So come on, let's leave the preschool finger-painting exercises on Christ and get on with the grand work of art. Grow up in Christ. The basic foundational truths are in place: turning your back on "salvation by self-help" and turning in trust toward God; baptismal instructions; laying on of hands; resurrection of the dead; eternal judgment. God helping us, we'll stay true to all that. But there's so much more. Let's get on with it!

What all of this is essentially saying is….GROW UP! It's time to move past playing with Barbie dolls and toy airplanes, coloring books and crayons. There must be some advancement in our growth.

Well how do I know I'm maturing in Christ? I'm glad you asked. Here's a few signs that you're growing and maturing in Christ.

1. **When you begin to mature in Christ your faith will be tried. Thru the trying of your faith, patience should be the end result.**

   James 1:2-4 *3Knowing this, that the trying of your faith worketh patience. 4But let patience have her perfect work, that ye may be perfect and entire, wanting nothing.*

2. **You will treat other people right.**

   James 2:8 - *If ye fulfill the royal law according to the scripture, Thou shalt love neighbor as thyself, ye do well:*

Your tongue will be disciplined. You won't entertain or incite gossip. You will only speak of those things that are true. For we know that within the tongue lies the power of life and death. You can either kill someone with your words or uplift them. Gossip should not be a part of your daily life if you're maturing in Christ.

Psalms 34:13 - *Keep thy tongue from evil and thy lips from speaking guile.*

3. **A mature person has a peaceful and non-violent nature.**

   James 4:1(Message) - *Where do you think all these appalling wars and quarrels come from? Do you think they just happen? Think again. They come about because you want your own way, and fight for it deep inside yourselves. You lust for what you don't have and are willing to kill to get it. You want what isn't yours and will risk violence to get your hands on it.*

4. **You will lead a life of prayer and supplication. You will pray for your haters and drama makers. You will pray for those who do you wrong.**

   Luke 6:28 - *Bless them that curse you, and pray for them which despitefully use you.*

5. **You will be able to put your past behind you, and let go of those things that do not glorify and uplift Christ. You'll be able to eulogize and bury your past; focusing only on what's to come. Your focus will be completely on God.**

Philippians 3:14 - *[13]Brethren, I count not myself to have apprehended: but this one thing I do, forgetting those things which are behind, and reaching forth unto those things which are before, [14]I press toward the mark for the prize of the high calling of God in Christ Jesus.*

These are just a few signs of growth and maturity in Christ. In order to mature we must examine the substance we are consuming. What is substance? Substance is the basic elements from which something can be developed. It is the quality of qualities that make a thing what it is. In order for a thing to be evident it must have substance.

You should have something to show for the years and years of work and dedication that you've put forth which in turn becomes a concrete foundation upon which to build.

Before a baby is born, his or her life supply is dependent upon what the mother consumes. Once the baby is born its primary food source for the first few months is either formula or breast milk. Eventually, this form of substance will no longer be enough to sustain or gratify the baby's hunger. Gradually different foods are introduced to the baby. As a baby's appetite intensifies so should our appetite for the word of God intensify. Babies do not remain babies…they transition from one stage to the next. We too should also transform spiritually from one level to the next level.

Advancing in the word of God is critical and we must incorporate fasting and prayer along with praise and worship. Doing so will only increase our level of maturity in Christ. Unfortunately, there are those who shy away from spiritual maturity because they are fully aware that when much is given much is required. Accountability factors itself in and there are some who do not want to become accountable for their actions or their growth. Instead they are content with having pocket change knowledge; just enough to get by on and to bypass being accountable to produce more. In order to build spiritual substance you must rid yourselves of things and people that are not instrumental in your walk with Christ. In the natural we eat food to sustain us, to help our physical bodies grow and mature. It is a known fact that we should have a bowel movement after each meal we digest. When we do not have regular bowel movements, we become constipated. Constipation is not good on our bodies. It weakens our immune system and can lead to a blockage in our bowels which is very painful.

It is no different in the spirit realm. Feeding ourselves the right stuff is only part of spiritual growth and maturity. The other part requires us to have what I call spiritual bowel movements. Sometimes it's vitally important for us as Christians to rid ourselves of anything that is contrary to the word of God. We are to examine our lives on a daily basis and delete, dismiss and deny anything that is not lined up with the word of God. If we don't do this we become spiritually constipated which weakens our spiritual immune system.

I challenge everyone that professes Christ as their Lord and Savior to seek God with great tenacity. Grab hold of the word of God and inject it into your heart and mind and then practice what you've digested. You will never have an intimate (close) relationship with anyone unless you spend quality time with that person. When you spend quality time with God, you begin to take on His characteristics. Your lifestyle will change. Your conversation will change. Your circle of friends will change. Remember, maturity in Christ is vitally important to being complete and perfect in Him.

PRAYER OF EMPOWERMENT:

Father, I commit my life to you. I surrender my ways to you. I acknowledge that in order for me to grow and mature in you I must commit myself to daily study of your word. My desire is to be complete in you God. I understand that requires action on my part. I'm hungry and thirsty for more knowledge. I need more of you God. I commit to dismissing from my life anything that is contrary to what your word says. I let go of the past and I press toward what is ahead of me, for in doing so I know my reward shall be great. I commit myself to growth and maturity in you. I acknowledge that I am no longer a child and that it's time for me to put away childish things and grow in grace in the nurture and admonition of you. Amen

"IDENTITY"

"Knowing Who You Are in Christ"

It is imperative that we know who we are in Christ, because the enemy desires to infiltrate our minds with lies and deception about who we really are. It is his full time job to trick the believer into believing he or she is not who they think they are. We need to learn who we are in Christ and confess it openly as an affirmation daily. It's important to know that you are who God says you are regardless of how you feel about yourself. We need to view ourselves in the truth of God's word and realize that who I am is not based upon how I feel the opinions of others. I am who God says I am.

Let's begin affirming who we are in Christ by following these simple truths:

- I am a child of God. John 1:12

But as many as received him, to them gave he power to become the sons of God, even to them that believe on his name:

- I am God's friend. James 2:23

And the scripture was fulfilled which saith, Abraham believed God, and it was imputed unto him for righteousness: and he was called the Friend of God.

- I am an Ambassador. 2 Corinthians 5:20

Now then we are ambassadors for Christ, as though God did beseech you by us: we pray you in Christ's stead, be ye reconciled to God.

- I am chosen. Ephesians 1:4

According as he hath chosen us in him before the foundation of the world, that we should be holy and without blame before him in love:

- I am God's workmanship. Ephesians 2:10

For we are his workmanship, created in Christ Jesus unto good works, which God hath before ordained that we should walk in them.

- I am more than a conqueror. Romans 8:37

Nay, in all these things we are more than conquerors through him that loved us.

Now let's affirm what God has already done for us...

- I have been redeemed by the blood. Revelations 5:9

And they sung a new song, saying, Thou art worthy to take the book, and to open the seals thereof: for thou wast slain, and hast redeemed us to God by thy blood out of every kindred, and tongue, and people, and nation;

- I have been set free from sin & condemnation. Romans 8:1-2

There is therefore now no condemnation to them which are in Christ Jesus, who walk not after the flesh, but after the Spirit.

For the law of the Spirit of life in Christ Jesus hath made me free from the law of sin and death.

- I have been justified freely by his grace. Romans 3:24

Being justified freely by his grace through the redemption that is in Christ Jesus.

- I have been given authority over the power of the enemy. Luke 10:19

Behold, I give unto you power to tread on serpents and scorpions, and over all the power of the enemy: and nothing shall by any means hurt you.

- I have been given access to God. Ephesians 3:12

In whom we have boldness and access with confidence by the faith of him.

And because God has given us power, access and authority, let us apply these affirmations of what we "CAN" do in our lives.

- I can do all things through Christ which strengtheneth me. Phil 4:13
- I can come boldly to the throne of grace. Hebrews 4:16
- I can declare liberty to the captives. Isaiah 61:1
- I can tread on serpents. Luke 10:19
- I can pray always and everywhere. Luke 21:36
- I can resist the devil and he will flee. James 4:7

These are just a few of the many affirmations found in the Word of God. Take time to delve deeper in the word to discover your true "Identity" in Christ. The enemy is on his job to rob you of your true identity, so we must be on our jobs to ensure we confess daily who we are in Christ, and the authority he has given us to overcome the enemy.

PRAYER OF EMPOWERMENT:

Father as I study your word, show me who I am, what I have access to, and what I have authority over. Teach me who I am in you. Show me my "true" identity. Empower me to resist the devil and his plots to infiltrate my mind with negative images and descriptions of who I am. Empower me to affirm the word of truth in and over my life. Empower me to encourage others to affirm the truth of your word in their lives. Let the word of God be a mirror image of who I am in you. Amen.

PEARLS OF WARNING

R-E-S-P-E-C-T

"Stop Playing With Me"

SCRIPTURAL EMPHASIS:

[6] The LORD of Heaven's Armies says to the priests: "A son honors his father, and a servant respects his master. If I am your father and master, where are the honor and respect I deserve? You have shown contempt for my name! "But you ask, 'How have we ever shown contempt for your name?' [7] "You have shown contempt by offering defiled sacrifices on my altar. "Then you ask, 'How have we defiled the sacrifices?' "You defile them by saying the altar of the LORD deserves no respect.

Upon close observation, the majority of the church has lost its respect for the Lord. Where there was once great reverence for the Lord, it has now been replaced with blatant disregard of His sovereignty and Lordship. We enter the house of God as wild animals on the attack. Respect for leadership and authority is becoming a distant memory. Instead of being a force to build up the Kingdom of God, it has taken a nasty turn for the worse and now what was once built up is being torn down and sadly by some of the same ones that aided in building it up. We confess Christ as our Lord and Savior, but where is our respect and reverence for Him? There used to be a time that we were afraid to sin or do wrong. We would be so convicted if we fell from grace. Now sin has become a practice for many. Now anything goes and it's being accepted in a vast majority of the churches across the nation.

There's a newfound doctrine that is sweeping the land. The diseased doctrine or gospel of inclusion is being spread and accepted by many. This doctrine teaches these points:

- The death of Jesus Christ on the cross and His resurrection paid the price for all of humanity to have eternal life in heaven, <u>without any requirement to repent of sins and receive salvation.</u>

- Belief in Jesus Christ <u>is not necessary for a person to go to heaven.</u> Salvation is unconditional, granted by the grace of God to every human being.

- It is presumed that <u>all of humanity will have its destiny in heaven</u>, whether they realize it or not.

- <u>All of humanity will go to heaven regardless of their religious affiliation, including those who believe in false religions or adopt any other form of religious persuasion, or who have no religious persuasion.</u>

- Only those who have "tasted of the fruits" of real intimacy with Christ and have "intentionally and consciously rejected" the grace of God will spend eternity separated from God.

- There are persons in some type of hell, <u>but the emphasis is "to get away from the picture of an angry, intolerant God. I don't see God that bitter."</u>

This doctrine is blatantly disrespectful and it desecrates the true meaning of the Word of God. It has taken the true unadulterated Word of God and made mockery of it. The sad

part is that many have fallen for this hypocrisy. The Bible speaks in 2 Timothy 4:3 (NLT)

³ For a time is coming when people will no longer listen to sound and wholesome teaching. They will follow their own desires and will look for teachers who will tell them whatever their itching ears want to hear.

It is important to note that God does not change His standards for anyone. Malachi 3:6a (KJV) states, *⁶For I am the LORD, I change not;*

James 1:17 tells us *"Every good gift and every perfect gift is from above and comes down from the Father of lights, with whom is no variableness nor shadow of turning." The shadow of turning relates to the sun which eclipses, and turns, and casts its shadow. It rises and sets, appears and disappears every day; and it comes out of one tropic, and enters into another at certain seasons of the year. But with God, who is light itself, there is no darkness at all; there is no change, nor anything like it. He is unchangeable in His nature, perfections, purposes, promises, and gifts. He is holy and he cannot turn to anything evil; nor can He, the light of the world, be the reason or cause of darkness, and since every good and perfect gift comes from Him, evil cannot proceed from him, nor can he tempt any to it.*

The Bible is very clear that God does not and will not change His mind, His will, or His nature. The word of God is settled in Heaven. (Psalms 119:89)

God is not pleased with the state of the church in its current state. From contrary doctrines to just blatant disrespect for Him and the things of God; God is not pleased.

Those who profess Christ are living their lives as if God does not exist. They say they love God but yet their lifestyle tells a

different story. They say they are born again, baptized, spirit filled believers but again their lifestyles are totally contrary to the word of God. They talk about living a holy and righteous lifestyle but its mere words because their actions prove otherwise.

2 Corinthians 7:1 tells us to separate ourselves from anything that is unclean as a sign of reverence to God. Let us take a look at this scripture in depth in the New Living Translation; [1] *Because we have these promises, dear friends, let us cleanse ourselves from everything that can defile our body or spirit. And let us work toward complete holiness because we fear God.*

The Bible also tells us in, 1 Peter 1:16, Because it is written, Be ye holy; for I am holy.

The word of God goes on to say in 1 Thessalonians 4:7-8 (Amplified), [7]*For God has not called us to impurity but to consecration [to dedicate ourselves to the most thorough purity].* [8]*Therefore whoever disregards (sets aside and rejects this) disregards not man but God, Whose [very] Spirit [Whom] He gives to you is holy (chaste, pure).*

It grieves me to see how many are falling into diver temptations and falling for false doctrines. The church is losing ground by losing its reverence for God. When we were in the world and living according to the doctrine of satan, we had no problem showing up to the club or the party on time. We would make sure that we were primped and primed; ready to go out and support the cause of satan. We would lay out our clothes and plan days in advance, but when it comes to showing up to the house of God; we show up drastically late or not at all. We have a million excuses why we can't attend the worship services. We'll use weak excuses like I have nothing to wear or I don't have a ride or gas money, but when we wanted to get to the club we had our transportation arrangements confirmed well in advance. And then there are those who after partying all night long; will enter into the house of God still wreaking of liquor and cigarette smoke from the night before; having the bold audacity to step on the platform to lead. No respect for God or the house of God….having a form of godliness but denying the power. We've become experts at playing church. But God is issuing a warning, "Stop playing with me". "Show some respect". God will not receive your defiled sacrifices.

How can you fix your mouth to ask God for anything when you can't show Him the reverence He deserves? When we get in trouble we run to Him, begging and pleading Him to help us. But when things are going well we can't be found worshipping or praising Him. We want God to bless us with financial prosperity, but we fail to pay our tithes and offer up a sacrifice with our offering. Stop playing with God!

God is not a slot machine. God cannot be pimped. You can't just run to God when you're in trouble but when all is well He never hears your voice. Show some respect to the one who has the power to breathe the breath of life in your body another day or cause you to cease from breathing. Show some respect to the one, true, living and holy God. He deserves and commands respect. God doesn't play games with us so we are not to play games with Him. Time is winding up and we are to be about our Father's business. God's return is imminent. It's time to get serious about God and serve Him with true diligence. God is not a chess piece that you can move as you see fit. God cannot be played or toyed with. God is not under our control, but we should be under His control. He has the keys to life and death in His hand. He has all power and authority. Wake up before God says to you, "Game Over"….depart from me you who work iniquity for I know you not.

PRAYER OF EMPOWERMENT:

Father, forgive us for playing games with you. Forgive us for defiling your temple. Forgive us for taking you for granted. Father, help us to live according to the scriptures. Forgive us for lending our ear to false doctrine from slick and perverse lips. Father, help us to live according to your purpose and plan. Father, empower us to become a people that have your heart and your mind. Strengthen us to withstand the wiles and tactics of the enemy. Lord, empower us to separate ourselves from anything or anyone that is not like you. Forgive us God. Let our lives be an example of your saving grace, love & mercy. Lord, convict us when we do wrong and let us be found in a repentant stance when we fall. Lord, empower us to be obedient to your word. Empower us according to Ephesians 4:1-6 (paraphrased), to walk worthy of the vocation wherewith we have been called. Let us walk with lowliness, meekness and longsuffering. Help us to forbear one another in love. Let our endeavor be to keep the unity of the Spirit in the bond of peace. Let us be forever mindful that there is one body, and one Spirit, even as we are called in one hope of your calling; One Lord, one faith, one baptism, one God and Father of all, who is above all, and through all, and in us all.

Amen

WAKE UP ZION!
THE LORD'S RETURN IS NEAR!

SCRIPTURAL EMPHASIS:

Mark 13:32-37 (King James Version)

[32]But of that day and that hour knoweth no man, no, not the angels which are in heaven, neither the Son, but the Father. [33]Take ye heed, watch and pray: for ye know not when the time is. [34]For the Son of Man is as a man taking a far journey, who left his house, and gave authority to his servants, and to every man his work, and commanded the porter to watch. [35]Watch ye therefore: for ye know not when the master of the house cometh, at even, or at midnight, or at the cockcrowing, or in the morning: [36]Lest coming suddenly he find you sleeping. [37]And what I say unto you I say unto all, Watch.

It's time to get back to God. I mean really get back to God. It's time for our focus to be returned to living a lifestyle of Holiness. I'm truly grieved in my spirit at how church has become so secular. How we no longer live by a standard of holiness. How we just willingly accept anything. Our motto has become "Anything goes" instead of "Holiness or Hell". We can't get angry when the church is now known as a social network. We can't get angry at the "Club" atmosphere that is now so prevalent in churches all across the world. Especially when we allow anything to be viewed in our homes, anything to be played in our cars and when we have more mental retention of the latest Rap, Rock, or R&B lyrics than we have of what the word of God says.

Then we wonder why our youth have no TRUE identity. We wonder why our youth have no interest in serving God. How is it okay for a man or woman of God (an alleged one that is) to drink, smoke, club, fornicate, curse, commit adultery, lie, steal, cheat, backbite, gossip, and do these things openly; then we see these very same people teaching bible study, singing in the choir, working the altar, here's one...Training our children??? And then we have the audacity to try and justify our sinful ways by saying we have to meet the world where they are. We have to get on their level to pull them up. Pull them up to what? Knowing how to be a professional impersonator of a Kingdom Heir? Are you serious?

Then there are those who want to flip it by saying that when they're called out for their mess, that's its being judgmental. The oldest cop out in the book used to aide in continuing in a sinful lifestyle. How dare you call yourself a man or woman of God? How dare you say you're a part of the lineage of Christ? How can your identity be in Christ when you're playing both sides; living completely contrary to the word of God. Christ did not win the world by becoming like the world. NO! On the contrary, He wrapped himself in flesh, dwelling among all people, yet he didn't become acquainted with sin. He didn't practice sin so he could draw sinners from sin. He didn't use the tactics of the world to draw the world. No! He walked upright before all men. And that's how He expects us to live. There's no compromising the word of God. God is not pleased and his wrath is about to fall on every house that stands contrary to the word of God. Will the TRUE church of the living God please stand up? Wake up Zion! For the Lord's return is near.

Our churches need to go through spiritual rehab because they're high and doped up on fame and fortune. Our churches are in a demonic trance; captivated and mesmerized by the secular world; addicted to the glam and glitz that the world dangles before their eyes. Our churches are hypnotized by secular advancement. Hidden agendas raping the community; but they label it outreach and soul winning. They are more concerned about seat filling than soul winning. Preachers tallying up how many people their churches are running instead of how many souls ran to the altar crying out, what must I do to be saved? No longer do we have revival meetings, tent crusades, or bona fide deliverance services where so many of us reading this were saved, set free and delivered. Now it's Mega Conferences with attached price tags so high you have to apply for a loan to attend. Wake up Zion! The Lord's return is near.

I remember growing up hearing the Mothers of the church sing a song that says, "O Zion what's the matter now?" You don't pray like you used to pray...What's the matter now? You don't sing like you used to sing...What's the matter now?...You don't walk like you used to walk...What's the matter now?...You don't talk like you used to talk...What's the matter now? I'm sorry but I'm a firm believer that what it took back then...it takes the same today. The spiritual manifestation that took place on Azusa Street back in April of 1906 is the same experience we should all continuously seek.

When did self gratification become more important than having a genuine and sincere intimate relationship with God? What happened to the standard of Holiness? I'm not talking about some man-made version of Holiness, but I'm talking about the standard that Christ set.

1 Peter 1:13-19 (NIV) says,
13 Therefore, prepare your minds for action; be self-controlled; set your hope fully on the grace to be given you when Jesus Christ is revealed. 14 as obedient children do not conform to the evil desires you had when you lived in ignorance. 15 but just as he who called you is holy, so be holy in all you do; 16 for it is written: "Be holy, because I am holy."

17 Since you call on a Father, who judges each man's work impartially, live your lives as strangers here in reverent fear. 18 For you know that it was not with perishable things such as silver or gold that you were redeemed from the empty way of life handed down to you from your forefathers, 19 but with the precious blood of Christ, a lamb without blemish or defect.

Why have we allowed the Word of God to be mutilated and dissected? Why do we treat the Word of God like a nursery rhyme or fairy tale? What is really going on? We don't defend the word like we should...instead we'll allow folk that say they are Prophet, Evangelist, Bishop, Minister, Elder, Reverend, and even those without a title to come and release a word over the people of God only to hear a watered down feel good message sprinkled with a few scriptures here and there or many times no scripture at all. The church has become nothing more than a feeding frenzy for those who just need a feel good pick me up sermon that will help them justify their sinful week long deeds not to mention the drunken stupor they were in the night before (many times hours before) they enter into the house of God.

Everything goes now....we've gotten so far from preaching the gospel the way it is written and the way God intended. We teach our young people that listening to secular music is okay...that watching filthy and lewd movies is okay...that going to clubs and parties is okay....just as long as you come to church on Sunday and repent. What!!!!! Are you serious? But wait...Now the club is in the church...the same music you hear in the club, BET, MTV, VHI and every other secular avenue is now featured...(Check this out) IN THE CHURCH. Oh but that's not it...we now have hip hop dance teams in THE CHURCH....so now we've made it okay for our young people to come in the church dropping it like it's hot. And then on top of all of that....we allow young and old to come in the house of God dressed like they're headed for the club or the street corner. Cleavage hanging out, clothes so tight that every part of their anatomy is on public display. Yeah, I know it's tight...but it's also RIGHT. And then we have the audacity to try and call out folk who are really striving to live right. We make fun of the ones who truly have a heart for God...Why? Because we choose not to conform to the world...because we choose to "STAND UP" and "STAND OUT". Oh and hold on those of you who think I too have not been found guilty of any of this foolishness, because sadly enough I've found myself in a state of conformity too. I just decided to WAKE UP, STAND UP, and SPEAK UP. I'm not scared of the devil and I will not hold my peace any longer. We're living in the last days in case you all didn't know. Things that were spoken that would happen in the last days are happening. The very ELECT are being deceived. I'm tired of this mentality of "just go along with the flow". Some may even ask, what can you do about it? I'll tell you what you and I can do about it. We can bombard Heaven, calling out and rebuking this modern day Christianity. We can fall on our knees and pray until something happens. We have the POWER to bind and loose. We no longer have to deal with it and just go along with it…So please stop talking about it and BE about it.

Matthew 16:18-19 says,
18 And I say also unto thee, that thou art Peter, and upon this rock I will build my church; and the gates of hell shall not prevail against it.
19 And I will give unto thee the keys of the kingdom of heaven: and whatsoever thou shalt bind on earth shall be bound in heaven: and whatsoever thou shalt loose on earth shall be loosed in heaven.

The last days are being fulfilled….RIGHT NOW!!!!!!

2 Timothy 3 (KJV)

1 This know also, that in the last days perilous times shall come.
2 For men shall be lovers of their own selves, covetous, boasters, proud, blasphemers, disobedient to parents, unthankful, unholy,
3 Without natural affection, trucebreakers, false accusers, incontinent, fierce, despisers of those that are good,
4 Traitors, heady, high-minded, lovers of pleasures more than lovers of God;
5 Having a form of godliness, but denying the power thereof: from such turn away.
6 For of this sort are they which creep into houses, and lead captive silly women laden with sins, led away with divers lusts,
7 Ever learning, and never able to come to the knowledge of the truth.
8 Now as Jannes and Jambres withstood Moses, so do these also resist the truth: men of corrupt minds, reprobate concerning the

faith. 9 But they shall proceed no further: for their folly shall be manifest unto all men, as their's also was.

10 But thou hast fully known my doctrine, manner of life, purpose, faith, longsuffering, charity, patience,

11 Persecutions, afflictions, which came unto me at Antioch, at Iconium, at Lystra; what persecutions I endured: but out of them all the Lord delivered me.

12 Yea, and all that will live godly in Christ Jesus shall suffer persecution.

13 But evil men and seducers shall wax worse and worse, deceiving, and being deceived.

14 But continue thou in the things which thou hast learned and hast been assured of, knowing of whom thou hast learned them;

15 And that from a child thou hast known the holy scriptures, which are able to make thee wise unto salvation through faith which is in Christ Jesus.

16 All scripture is given by inspiration of God, and is profitable for doctrine, for reproof, for correction, for instruction in righteousness:

17 That the man of God may be perfect, thoroughly furnished unto all good works.

PRAYER OF EMPOWERMENT:

Father, forgive we your people for living contrary to your word. Forgive us for becoming more like the world and less like you. Forgive us for adorning ourselves with worldly standards and mentalities. Forgive us for conforming and fashioning ourselves after secular artist and movie stars. Forgive us for becoming so spiritually weak that we have forsaken the truth. Forgive us God. Forgive us. Forgive us for inverting our values. Forgive us for endorsing perversion, neglecting the needy, and exploiting the poor. Search us Lord and know our hearts. Cleanse us from every sin and free us according to your will. Transform us God into the man and woman of God you've ordained us to be. Prepare us for your return. Amen

IS YOUR VESSEL READY?

SCRIPTURAL EMPHASIS:

2 Timothy 2:21 (Amplified Bible)

21So whoever cleanses himself [from what is ignoble and unclean, who separates himself from contact with contaminating and corrupting influences] will [then himself] be a vessel set apart and useful for honorable and noble purposes, consecrated and profitable to the Master, fit and ready for any good work.

Before we can birth forth our individual purpose and callings we must first ensure that our vessels are ready. The above scripture notes that we must cleanse ourselves from anything that is unclean. It also states that we should separate ourselves from corrupt or contaminating influences.

We must prepare ourselves for the Master's use. The word of God tells us in Romans 12:1, *I beseech you therefore, brethren, by the mercies of God, that ye present your bodies a living sacrifice, holy, acceptable unto God, which is your reasonable service.*

We see in the scripture text that the Apostle Paul is making an appeal to the people. The word beseech signifies the intensity of this appeal. Paul is urging, pleading, begging the people to make a decisive dedication of their bodies to God. We are to devote ourselves to God and consecrate our lives for the Master's use.

Paul states it's our reasonable service. What he's saying is that it's not too much to ask one to do. It's a rational and intelligent decision to make.

The Message version of the bible states in Romans 12:1, So here's what I want you to do, God helping you: Take your everyday, ordinary life--your sleeping, eating, going-to-work, and walking-around life--and place it before God as an offering. Embracing what God does for you is the best thing you can do for him.

God wants total commitment. He wants a sacrificial offering to be representative of our love and devotion to Him. God wants us to recognize that we are nothing without Him. God wants us to clean house. What do I mean by that statement? God wants us to rid ourselves of anything and anyone that will prohibit or prevent us from obtaining what He has for us.

In order to birth forth our purpose, we must continually rid ourselves of unnecessary baggage. There may be some people in your life that you have to let go of. Understand that everyone does not have your best interest at heart. There are some people in your life that want to destroy and have you abort the purpose inside of you. These people have no vision, no aspirations or goals, and they want to hinder you because they see your potential. Some people are hanging around as leeches. They desire to suck the life out of you because they walk around lifeless and without purpose.

It's very important that you do not reveal your dreams, visions, and purpose to just anyone. There may be times where you can't tell anyone what God has shown you. It's at these times that you must trust and believe God for guidance and instruction. It can be detrimental to say the least if you reveal what God has shown you to the wrong person. Again, some people are out to destroy

you and not to encourage you. Be very careful who you share your dreams with.

Let's take a look in scripture. Genesis 37:14-20 (Amplified) says,

14And [Jacob] said to him, Go, I pray you, see whether everything is all right with your brothers and with the flock; then come back and bring me word. So he sent him out of the Hebron Valley, and he came to Shechem.

15And a certain man found him, and behold, he had lost his way and was wandering in the open country. The man asked him, What are you trying to find?

16And he said, I am looking for my brothers. Tell me, I pray you, where they are pasturing our flocks.

17But the man said, [They were here, but] they have gone. I heard them say, Let us go to Dothan. And Joseph went after his brothers and found them at Dothan.

18And when they saw him far off, even before he came near to them, they conspired to kill him.

19And they said one to another, See, here comes this dreamer and master of dreams.

20So come on now, let us kill him and throw his body into some pit; then we will say [to our father], some wild and ferocious animal has devoured him; and we shall see what will become of his dreams!

We see here in scripture that because Joseph possessed the gift of dreams, his own brothers sought to kill him. They didn't want to see him prosper. It's sad to think that your very own family may be seeking to destroy your destiny, but it's also very true. You must protect the gift, the calling; the purpose God has

impregnated you with, just as you would in the natural to protect your unborn child.

You must also ensure your heart remains pure before God. God always looks at your heart and the intent therein. He doesn't depend on what your mouth is saying, but he's listening to your heart. The intent of your heart determines the validity of your purpose.

PRAYER OF EMPOWERMENT:

Father, empower me to remain pure before you. Search my heart Lord and show me the intent and motives that are within. Lord, teach me how to maintain integrity and Christian character. Strengthen me Lord to protect the gifts that you've place on the inside of me. Let me birth forth your purpose and your plan for my life; tearing down selfish desires and hidden agendas. Lord, help me to not void out or abort my destined purpose by revealing the secret things you've shown me to wolves in sheep clothing. Amen

"A Killer is Among Us!"

Scriptural Emphasis:

The thief cometh not, but for to steal, and to kill, and to destroy: I am come that they might have life, and that they might have it more abundantly. John 10:10 (KJV)

The role of the enemy is clear. He exists merely to rob us from the abundant life God has already provided for us. Satan uses devices such as temptation to rob you of your rightful place in the Kingdom of God. Have you received an invitation from Satan lately to give up your place in the Kingdom of God for a place in his Kingdom? Trust me, his tactics will be cunning and crafty; most will not even recognize them. Temptation begins with an evil thought that is planted in the mind; if not immediately dismissed it will result in destruction. You cannot entertain these thoughts, but you must rebuke the very insinuation of sin.

Satan's job is to make sin look appealing. He'll paint an alluring masterpiece of his alleged kingdom to lure you in; but once he has you in his territory, what appeared to be a land of milk and honey will soon reveal its true landscape of Death and Destruction. What first appeared to be a land overflowing with rubies and diamonds; upon further inspection is that of muck and mire. Don't fall for what you see because what you see is not always what you see; looks are most times deceiving.

The enemy deceived Eve by tempting her with the expectation of being like God if only she would eat from the tree of knowledge. But what Eve failed to realize is that she was being lured into

102

doing something that was in total defiance of what God had said. In essence, he was saying if you want to be like God you must defy the authority of God and do what you want to do. Do not be deceived by this tactic. The only way to be more like God is to obey God. Satan's fall from Heaven took place because he wanted the power of God. He wanted to be higher than God and he wanted to control the Kingdom of God. Defying God will only cause you to be destroyed and your kingdom status forfeited.

There are three critical areas of temptation: (1) physical desires, (2) material possessions and authority (power), (3) Pride.

Let's break these three areas of interest down further.

In studying Matthew 4:1-10 which involves Satan's attempt to tempt Jesus, we see here that Jesus, who had been fasting for forty days and nights, would by all accounts at this point be physically hungry and desirous of food. However Satan attempt to tempt Jesus with tangible food failed miserably. Christ instead rebuked the enemy by telling him that man should does not live by bread alone, but by every word that proceeds out of the mouth of God.

After failing to tempt Jesus with bread, Satan again attempts to tempt Jesus by taking him to the highest point of the temple in the holy city commanding that if he is indeed the Son of God to throw himself down so that the angels will rescue him causing his feet not to touch or strike a stone. Christ once again stood toe to toe with the enemy declaring that it is written, do not put the Lord your God to the test. Here we see the enemy trying to tempt Christ to put his power and authority to the test.

Finally, the enemy tries to tempt Christ one last time by taking Him up to a high mountain; showcasing the splendor of the kingdoms of the world; offering it all to Christ if only He would bow down and worship him. By this time Jesus was clearly tired of the enemy and his foolish attempts to tempt Him, so he told the devil to get away from him and worship the Lord and serve Him only. What baffles me is how the enemy thought he could offer what already belongs to God. But that's just how weak-minded the enemy is. Satan can't give what he doesn't possess; everything belongs to God.

The bible clearly instructs the people of God to run from temptation. I know that some may think that running is a sign of weakness, but in reality it's a sign of strength. Sometimes it's imperative that you distance yourself or remove yourself completely from certain situations to keep you from falling into temptation. The bible tells us if we resist the devil, he will flee.

Flee the evil desires of youth, and pursue righteousness, faith, love and peace, along with those who call on the Lord out of a pure heart. Knowing when to flee and when to fight is instrumental in spiritual warfare. (2 Timothy 2:22)

There's a killer among us…and his name is Satan! He's seeking those he can destroy and devour. Remain vigilant and watchful, sober in mind so that when temptation comes you will be able to endure and overcome.

Blessed is the man that endures temptation: for when he is tried, he shall receive the crown of life, which the Lord hath promised to them that love him. (James 1:12)

PRAYER OF EMPOWERMENT:

Father I pray that you will empower me to withstand the tricks, tactics and schemes of the enemy. Lord as I obey your word, grant me the wisdom to recognize the attack of the enemy. Forgive me for the times that I've yielded myself to the enemy. Lord help me to be vigilant, watchful and prayerful; that I will not fall for the devices of the enemy; for as I endure temptation I know that when I am tried I will receive the crown of life which you have promised. Amen

THE ALLURE OF DECEPTION

SCRIPTURAL EMPHASIS:

Matthew 24:4-5 (Amplified Bible)

⁴Jesus answered them, Be careful that no one misleads you [deceiving you and leading you into error]. ⁵For many will come in (on the strength of) My name appropriating the name which belongs to Me], saying, I am the Christ (the Messiah), and they will lead many astray.

I feel compelled to share what has been plaguing my mind and grieving my spirit. There seems to be an epidemic of our spiritual leaders either falling from grace or being found in compromising positions. This has been in my opinion detrimental to the Body of Christ. I will not speak against any leader nor do I have an opinion or speculation on their guilt or innocence. All I can and will continue to do is pray that deliverance and restoration take place in their lives. But whenever there is a scandal within the body of Christ, great controversy emerges.

Let me first begin by saying, the Word of God is and will always be truth. It is a truth that requires no defense. I have been agitated to say the least with the emergence of those who have come out trying to twist and manipulate the word of God by trying to persuade the Body of Christ that we should embrace the homosexual lifestyle. Now I in no way will ever bash anyone

for their choices, but I also will never accept this lifestyle of perversion. It's the sin I abhor not the person held in its captivity.

What baffles me is while the world is pushing this agenda for Christianity to be all inclusive; the Church is sitting on the sidelines paralyzed with muted lips, deaf ears, and blinded eyes. Well, enough is enough. Will the radical men and women of God please stand up? It's time to cry aloud and spare not. Where is the voice of the Church?

The church has become way too secular. When did it become okay for women to enter into God's house with everything showing and nothing hidden? Now it's acceptable for women to come in with their cleavage on display and their clothes so tight that one can label every part of her anatomy? When did it become okay for men, young and old to enter into the sanctuary pants sagging to their knees and underwear fully exposed? What has happened to our reverence for the house of God? Instead of the church drawing the world; the world is now luring the church. We've altered our services to entertain the audience. It's all a big performance now. We've constructed sanctuaries to resemble the club...flashing lights, disco balls and smoke machines. Praise and Worship has become nothing more than a performance of puppets on a string; all flash but no anointing; tinkling brass and clanging cymbals. We allow witches and warlocks to preach in the pulpit, feel good tell the people what they want to hear; non-offensive, have it your way sermons. We don't want to offend anyone fearing they will leave the church taking their financial support along with them. Hell is no longer preached...the wages of sin is no longer preached. What happened to the church being a hospital for the sick? What happened to this being about souls saved, lives changed, habits broken, addictions delivered and bodies healed? The church has developed a form of godliness but denies the very power of God.

God is not pleased with the church and that's why sin is being exposed. God has begun to spew this lukewarm version of Christianity out of His mouth. The church is covered in phlegm. It's infected with sin and God is tired of it. It's time for the radical believers to stand up and speak out. We've sat in silence long enough. It's Holiness or Hell; Life or Death…either you're in or you're out; hot or you're cold because everything lukewarm is about to be expelled from the Body of Christ.

I will not accept this new contemporary version of Christianity. Inclusion is not an option and it's not biblical. I will not fall prey to the seducing nature of this world. I was once in sin…I've fallen and made many mistakes, done things that I regret, but I thank God for not turning His back on me, and the debt I owe Him is my life….totally and completely surrendered for His use and His use only. I choose to be on the winning side, and I refuse to succumb to the demonic forces of this world. I will stand up, cry loud and proclaim Christ. I will tell this dying world to turn from their wicked ways or hell will be their resting place because the wages of sin is death. I can't make compromises with the world.

The world has seduced and deceived the church long enough. The Bible says that the very elect will be deceived. We are living in perilous times. The Bible says in, 2 Timothy 3:1-5 (Message Version) Don't be naive. There are difficult times ahead. As the end approaches, people are going to be self-absorbed, money-hungry, self-promoting, stuck-up, profane, contemptuous of parents, crude, coarse, dog-eat-dog, unbending, slanderers, impulsively wild, savage, cynical, treacherous, ruthless, bloated windbags, addicted to lust, and allergic to God. They'll make a show of religion, but behind the scenes they're animals. Stay clear of these people.

God is trying to warn us, but we've turned a deaf ear, because truth is no longer popular. Instead we'd rather listen to things that tickle our ears and caress our flesh. Please note, if you are a practitioner of sin you will not enter Heaven's gates.

The Word of God warns us over and over again about deception. In 2 Corinthians 11:2-4 it speaks about being deceived into worshipping other gods and following another gospel.

In 1 Corinthians 6:8-10 it tells us not to be deceived in thinking that the unrighteous will inherit the kingdom of God.

In 1 Corinthians 15:33-34 it tells us that we are to not be deceived into thinking that it's okay to hang out with practitioners of sin because evil company will corrupt good habits.

Galatians 6:7-8 warns us about mocking God. Whatever we sow; we shall reap. If you sow corruption you will reap corruption.

Again in Galatians 5:19-21 we are warned if we continue practicing sin we will not inherit the kingdom of God.

All throughout the word of God we see where it is instructed that we should not allow ourselves to be deceived.

Ephesians 5:6a –Let no man deceive you with vain words.

1 John 3:7-8 - 7 *Little children, let no man deceive you: he that doeth righteousness is righteous, even as he is righteous. 8 He that committeth sin is of the devil; for the devil sinneth from the beginning. For this purpose the Son of God was manifested, that he might destroy the works of the devil.*

I can go on and on, but let me leave this last scripture: Jude 2-4
²Mercy unto you, and peace, and love, be multiplied.

³Beloved, when I gave all diligence to write unto you of the common salvation, it was needful for me to write unto you, and exhort you that ye should earnestly contend for the faith which was once delivered unto the saints.

⁴For there are certain men crept in unawares, who were before of old ordained to this condemnation, ungodly men, turning the grace of our God into lasciviousness, and denying the only Lord God, and our Lord Jesus Christ.

The Word of God is truth...and again it needs no defense. It's the truth all by itself. The Body of Christ must wipe the sleep from its eyes and wake up. We don't have time to sit back and relax...but we must be about kingdom business...our Fathers business. We must reclaim our strength and authority and stand for righteousness.

PRAYER OF EMPOWERMENT:

Father, I ask that you destroy and remove deception from the minds of your people. I pray that you will expose and bring to shame everyone that is living contrary to your word yet confessing holiness. Lord, bless us with a sound mind and spirit. Destroy the plans, schemes and plots of the enemy to deceive and turn away the people of God. I pray that every form of deception be driven out of the Body of Christ. I pray that those who are operating in deception, witchcraft, sorcery, & magic be exposed. Father, empower us to be wise to the deception of the enemy and let us daily strengthen our spirit man through the word of God. Father, we reclaim our strength, our authority and our stand for righteousness. Amen

IT'S JUST STUFF!

SCRIPTURAL EMPHASIS:

For what is a man profited, if he shall gain the whole world, and lose his own soul? Or what shall a man give in exchange for his soul? Matthew 16:26

Today like never before we live in a society that tells you to buy now and pay later. Society pushes the belief that you can have whatever you want….NOW!!!

Have you ever been on your way to a department store and before you arrived you said you just wanted to window shop….but that fantasy passed quickly as soon as you walked inside the store. As long as you were outside the store you felt a little stronger to resist the temptation of spending, but once you stepped inside the store and was able to be up close and personal with the merchandise, that strength quickly dwindled and you found yourself calculating in your head what you could afford or how you could not pay your light bill and then double up next month.

Society is plastered with billboards, commercials, sale papers and internet sales. It's fascinating to me how we in one breath will say "I don't have any money" or "I'm saving up for a rainy day" until you see a new pair of shoes or electronic device you so

desperately want. Or that diamond bangle that you just have to have. Your savings have just become a thing of the past because you just can't say no.

Why are we as a people so materialistic? Why are we so fascinated with "stuff"? Why do we take on the motto, "More is better"…I have to get more? We worship our "things". We make them gods. We go out and purchase a new vehicle…bling it out and we now have to park two miles from our destination in fear of anyone scratching, denting or just breathing too closely to it. We dare someone to even look too closely at it.

What nonsense! It's funny how humble we were when we were catching the bus or riding the train or even better using the transportation God blessed us with…our feet. But now we won't even offer anyone a ride for fear of someone staining our seats or leaving smudges on the windows or door handles. And by all means I'm not suggesting we let anyone tear up what God has blessed us with, but realize that if God gave it to you, he will aid you in taking care of it. What audacity we have to act this way when if it were not for God we wouldn't have what we have.

It's sad how some people try to pimp God. They cry out in the late night hour when things are up in turmoil. When dark clouds rest on their foreheads they find themselves laying prostrate before God praying for relief. But as soon as God answers your cry….you stop praying, stop coming to church, stop reading your word, stop encouraging others, just stop in your tracks and act as if you've arrived. When things are going well and the money is flowing Oh how we love God, but as soon as things begin to take a turn for the worse and the repo man has come to take back what you turned into an idol to worship….we're ready then to curse God…falling out kicking and screaming.

The bible says, "For what is a man profited, if he shall gain the whole world, and lose his own soul? Or what shall a man give in exchange for his soul? Matthew 16:26

What profit is it to gain everything and then die with nothing? What profit is it to die and end up lifting up your eyes in hell? And what exactly are you willing to give up to get what you want? Would you lay down your very soul for materialistic gain?

Now hear me…It's nothing wrong with material gain. I strongly believe in prosperity. God desires for us to prosper. God wants us to have the best, but when you completely lose yourself in what you possess is when you go astray. Not only does God want us to prosper in the natural realm, but He said He also wants our soul to prosper.

Don't put your trust in things that will eventually return to dust, but put your forever trust in the God that created the dust and the things you possess. Give God the praise for the blessings you have been endowed with. Don't make your stuff your god. If we took as much time as we do caring for God and the things of God as we do our "stuff" what a better life we would possess. If we set our affection on things above what a difference this world would be. Salvation is the greatest possession one could ever have. Invite Christ into your life, seeking Him first and he will add to your life blessings that cannot be numbered.

PRAYER OF EMPOWERMENT:

Father, empower me to always bless you for who you are. I thank you for being my provision, but help me not to get caught up in the provision that I fail to bless you the provider of all things. Let my focus be on the prosperity of my spirit man. Help me to never get so consumed in material gain that I lose my focus on you. Lord, my complete trust is in you and not in things. Thank you for being Lord over my life. Amen

"KILL IT"

SCRIPTURAL EMPHASIS:

Those who belong to Christ Jesus have nailed the passions and desires of their sinful nature to his cross and crucified them there. (Galatians 5:24 NLT)

Successful Christian living requires us to walk not after the flesh but after the spirit. We cannot be effective in the Kingdom of God operating in the flesh. Within our flesh, lies no good thing. It is essential that we kill our flesh daily. How does one go about killing its flesh? You must be fully aware and knowledgeable of what your weaknesses are, and acknowledge them as such. We must deny ourselves of any pleasure that will lead us to sin and damnation; such as, fornication, evil communication, idolatry, adultery, witchcraft, hatred, envy, strife, drunkenness, gossip, back-biting, profanity, and so on.

In order to walk in the perfect will of God the flesh must die. You must dismiss and deny anything that will hinder your walk with Christ. Old relationships, soul ties, unhealthy friendships, habits, attitudes and addictions must be assassinated. Your flesh is the enemy of the spirit of God.

The sinful nature wants to do evil, which is just the opposite of what the Spirit wants. And the Spirit gives us desires that are the opposite of what the sinful nature desires. These two forces are constantly fighting each other, so you are not free to carry out your good intentions.(Galatians 5:17 NLT)

You cannot allow your flesh control over your spirit man. The spirit man must control your flesh. Your flesh will desire things that are pleasurable regardless of its sinful nature; but the spirit man must be strong enough to deny the flesh of these pleasures. The spirit will wake you up in the middle of the night to pray; but your flesh will say, "I'm too tired to get up". Your spirit will caution you to leave a certain individual alone; but your flesh will try and convince you there's nothing wrong with them. The spirit man will tell you to remain faithful with giving your tithes and offering; but your flesh will tell you to use it to buy a new outfit or pair of shoes. The spirit man and the flesh are constantly at battle. The flesh wants to annihilate your spirit. It wants complete control and total reign. Its job is to destroy you; but you must kill it before it kills you. Killing your flesh will bring life to your spirit man.

For if you live by its dictates, you will die. But if through the power of the Spirit you put to death the deeds of your sinful nature, you will live. (Romans 8:13 NLT)

We must condition our spirit man daily by prayer and meditating on the word of God. Just as any athlete must train its body before an athletic event or competition; we too must train and condition our spirit man to stand against the wiles, tactics, plots and schemes of the enemy.

I discipline my body like an athlete, training it to do what it should. Otherwise, I fear that after preaching to others I myself might be disqualified. (1 Corinthians 9:27 NLT)

Condemnation of past failures and errors cannot abide as long as we continue to walk after the spirit. Walking after the spirit frees you from the spirit of condemnation. The flesh desires you

to wallow in your past. The past wants you to be constantly reminded of your sins. The flesh does not want you to forget your sins; so it will always bring up what you used to do and who you used to be. The flesh will always resurrect the "You remember when" agenda. The flesh will try and convince you that it's so much more pleasurable to live in sin than it is to live for God. Don't be deceived by these tactics. We do not walk in condemnation as long as we belong to Christ.

There is therefore now no condemnation to them which are in Christ Jesus, who walk not after the flesh, but after the Spirit. (Romans 8:1 KJV)

Following your flesh and sinful nature will always lead to destruction and ultimately death. If you pursue the desires of the flesh, you will not inherit the Kingdom of God.

When you follow the desires of your sinful nature, the results are very clear: sexual immorality, impurity, lustful pleasures, [20] idolatry, sorcery, hostility, quarreling, jealousy, outbursts of anger, selfish ambition, dissension, division, [21] envy, drunkenness, wild parties, and other sins like these. Let me tell you again, as I have before, that anyone living that sort of life will not inherit the Kingdom of God. (Galatians 5:19-21 NLT)

When you walk after the spirit it produces certain attributes. The Holy Spirit is life! The Holy Spirit produces good fruit.

But the Holy Spirit produces this kind of fruit in our lives: love, joy, peace, patience, kindness, goodness, faithfulness, [23] gentleness, and self-control. There is no law against these things! (Galatians 5:22-23 NLT)

It is vitally important that you rid yourself of anything that is not like God. Anything that is contrary to the will, purpose and plan of God will lead you down the path of destruction. Sin is designed to kill. Sin offers a false appearance of pleasure. Just because it look, feel, sound, taste, and smell good; does not mean it's good for you. Sin is designed to be appealing to all of your senses, but it's merely a mirage. A person who is stranded in the desert for a long period of time without food, water or shelter from the heat will begin to see things that aren't there. Sin operates the same way. It dresses up to appeal to your senses. Again, you must rid yourself of anything that is not like God.

So get rid of all the filth and evil in your lives, and humbly accept the word God has planted in your hearts, for it has the power to save your souls. (James 1:21 NLT)

So get rid of all evil behavior. Be done with all deceit, hypocrisy, jealousy, and all unkind speech. (1Peter 2:1)

Never allow your emotions to dictate what you will and will not do. Always trust the leading and guidance of the Holy Spirit. Protect your spirit man. Demand and command your flesh to come under subjection. Encapsulate yourself in prayer and in the word of God. We are to present our bodies as living sacrifices to the Lord and live a holy lifestyle. Turn your flesh over to the Lord and let Him have His perfect work in you. Don't conform to worldly standards, but be transformed in your thinking so you will be fully aware of God's perfect will for your life.

I beseech you therefore, brethren, by the mercies of God, that ye present your bodies a living sacrifice, holy, acceptable unto God, which is your reasonable service.

²And be not conformed to this world: but be ye transformed by the renewing of your mind, that ye may prove what is that good, and acceptable, and perfect, will of God. (Romans 12:1-2 KJV)

PRAYER OF EMPOWERMENT:

Father, empower us to bring our flesh under subjection. Strengthen and empower us to not allow our flesh to rule or control our spirit man. Forgive us for yielding our members to sin. Forgive us for allowing our emotions to dictate our response and actions. Father, empower us to daily kill this flesh. Let us only yield to your spirit. Father empower us to not be conformed to this world, but to be transformed by the renewing of our minds. Let us be privy to the tactics, schemes and plots of the enemy. Let us not fall victim to those who resurrect our past in effort to bring condemnation upon us. Empower us to walk not after the flesh but after your spirit. Empower us to discipline and condition our bodies and our minds through daily study of your word. Thank you for dying on the cross for our sins and freeing us from the bondage of sin. Amen

ACCESS DENIED

SCRIPTURAL EMPHASIS:

Therefore, submit to God. Resist the devil and he will flee from you. (James 4:7)

We live in an age where anything and everything goes, but the sad part of it all is that this same mentality has infected those that confess Christ as their Lord and Savior. Nowadays it's hard to tell Kingdom people from worldly people. The church unfortunately has become too engulfed in reaching "mega" status that it has stooped to adopting some of the world's attitudes and characteristics. What's really unfortunate is that most that fall under this category don't realize the destruction that lies ahead of them if they continue adapting to the world versus trying to transform the world.

The Bible says that the people of God are to be a holy people, set apart, separate, unique, and peculiar. The word of God tells us that we should not conform ourselves to this world, but we are to be transformed by the renewing of our minds so we will be able to prove what is the good, acceptable, and perfect will of God for our lives. (See Romans 12:2)

The Bible clearly teaches us that we are not to fashion ourselves according to the world, but we are metamorphose into what God has called us to be. Our minds are to be renewed and renovated through the word of God.

Why would anyone want to conform to a world that one day will dissolve? The only thing that will be left intact is the word of God.

"Do not love the world or the things in the world. If anyone loves the world, the love of the Father is not in him. For all that is in the world -- the lust of the flesh, the lust of the eyes, and the pride of life -- is not of the Father but is of the world. And the world is passing away, and the lust of it; but he who does the will of God abides forever. (1 John 2:15-17 NKJV)

We the people of God are not of this world. We were handpicked out of the world by God. The world is not our friend, but on the contrary; it is our enemy.

If you were of the world, the world would love its own. Yet because you are not of the world, but I chose you out of the world, therefore the world hates you. (John 15:19 NKJV)

Because God redeemed us, purchased us with His blood we are no longer of this world. The world is actually our enemy. Why are we conforming ourselves to those who hate us?

You adulterers! Don't you realize that friendship with the world makes you an enemy of God? I say it again: If you want to be a friend of the world, you make yourself an enemy of God. (James 4:4 NLT)

So if we are friends with the world we hate God? Wow! What a powerful scripture. Why then do we befriend the world and conform to the things of the world knowing full well that the world hates us and that the world will one day be totally destroyed?

Proverbs 1:10 tell us, if sinners entice us we are not to consent. We are not to enter the path of the wicked, nor should we walk in the way of evil. We are to avoid it, not travel on it; turn away from it and pass on. (Proverbs 4:14)

All throughout the Bible, it clearly shows us that we are not to have any dealings with the world except to witness salvation to them. So why are we so quick to pick up the customs and traditions of the world? Why are we so overwhelmed and

engulfed with attaining fame, fortune and worldly notoriety? Why are we catering to the world with its tactics? Where is the separation? We the people of God are a peculiar people. We have been called out of darkness into the marvelous light of Jesus Christ.

We cannot do as the world does. We cannot live as the world does. We cannot fashion ourselves after the world. We are a holy nation...a royal priesthood. The world should be conforming to our standards. But we are too busy trying to get in good with those we feel can advance our agenda. We're too busy trying to gain the acceptance of man. We compromise our holy standards by allowing perverted men and women to release a word in our lives; tainted and flawed lips to sing on our Praise and Worship teams and in our choirs; sin afflicted hands playing on our instruments. We allow our children to pretty much do what they want to do. We've forsaken our foundation for fame; our vision for vices; our worship for wealth; our praise for perversion; and our standards for selfishness. We no longer take heed to sound doctrine, but we flock to Hollywood preachers and the mega church phenomenon's who only preach messages that please the flesh and stroke the egos of men.

God is not pleased with this type of lifestyle. Sadly these men and women think they are heaven bound, but according to Matthew 7:22-23 this is what the end resolve will be,

22 Many will say to me in that day, Lord, Lord, have we not prophesied in thy name? And in thy name have we cast out devils? And in thy name done many wonderful works?

23 And then will I profess unto them, I never knew you: depart from me, ye that work iniquity.

ACCESS DENIED!

PRAYER OF EMPOWERMENT:

Father, please do not deny us access into your Kingdom. Forgive us for trading our foundation for fame, our faith for fiction, our praise for pride, and our worship for wealth. Forgive us for seeking to please our flesh instead of seeking to please you. Empower us to walk upright before you. Strengthen us to take a stand for righteousness and to deny anything that is not like you. Lord I submit my life to your perfect will. Use me as you see fit for the advancing of the Kingdom and the edifying of the body of Christ. Transform my mind, create in me a clean heart, renew in me a right spirit, and restore me to my rightful place in you. AMEN

PEARLS OF EXPOSURE & ILLUMINATION

RELIGION VS SPIRITUALITY

SCRIPTURAL EMPHASIS:

Examine yourselves to see whether you are in the faith; test yourselves. Do you not realize that Christ Jesus is in you—unless, of course, you fail the test? (2 Corinthians 13:5 NIV)

Many people proclaim to be religious, but few profess spirituality. Religious people are those who have a personal set or institutionalized system of religious attitudes, beliefs, and practices.

Religion is anything that the individual practicing it desires it to be. Religion is defined by man which in turn is flesh manifested. Spirituality, however is God defined; therefore it is a clear and concrete representation of His nature. Religion because it is birthed and defined by man ultimately results in death but spirituality because it is birthed by God only leads to abundant living.

The very things we tend to put our focus and interest in; if it is not rooted in the Word of God...if not planted in the right soil...will not produce the right fruit and will ultimately bring death and destruction. But if we sow spiritual seed into fertile ground the result will produce fruit that will bear even more fruit.

Galatians 5:16-24 (NIV)

16 So I say, live by the Spirit, and you will not gratify the desires of the sinful nature. 17 For the sinful nature desires what is contrary to the Spirit and the Spirit what is contrary to the sinful nature. They are in conflict with each other, so that you do not do what you want. 18 But if you are led by the Spirit, you are not under law. 19 The acts of the sinful nature are obvious: sexual immorality, impurity and debauchery; 20 idolatry and witchcraft; hatred, discord, jealousy, fits of rage, selfish ambition, dissensions, factions 21 and envy; drunkenness, orgies, and the like. I warn you, as I did before, that those who live like this will not inherit the kingdom of God. 22 But the fruit of the Spirit is love, joy, peace, patience, kindness, goodness, faithfulness, 23 gentleness and self-control. Against such things there is no law. 24 Those who belong to Christ Jesus have crucified the sinful nature with its passions and desires.

The religious spirit is also commonly referred to as the spirit of Jezebel. The spirit of religion promotes doctrine contrary to the word of God. The spirit of religion attaches itself mainly to those who are new in the faith; those who have little knowledge depth in the Word of God. Identifying someone operating under the spirit of religion can be quite simple. They refuse to yield or submit to Christian authority and they live completely contrary to the Word of God. The spirit of religion makes its own standards and rules. This spirit is filthy and corrupt, and unfortunately once someone is operating under this spirit they become divisive, compromising, and manipulative. This spirit operates to destroy not to build up. Its purpose is to sow discord and cause division. Avoid this spirit!

Religious people regardless of their seemingly good nature and compassionate hearts, have the potential to hurt those who are striving to be spiritual with their negative words and attitudes. Religious people look down on, judge and try to antagonize those who don't share their same beliefs; dress in the same garments that they clothe themselves in, or simply see things the way they see things. Instead of being judgmental when we see our brother or sister overtaken in sin; we should pick them up, care for them, and help them return to the place of restoration. We should never place our foot on their necks; holding them hostage in guilt and condemnation. We must also remember that we were once sinners and if it were not for the grace of God, we would yet be in sin and hell bound.

We should strive to be like Christ; killing the very scent of religion; sowing good seed in good ground which will produce a Kingdom harvest. Our desire should be to have a deeper more intimate relationship with Christ, because relationship annihilates religion.

PRAYER OF EMPOWERMENT:

Father, in the Name of Jesus, I renounce the self consuming and disloyal spirit of religion. Empower me to refrain from engaging in this foul spirit. Shield me from all of its effects and divisive tactics, plots and schemes. Let my life be an example of your holiness! Father, saturate me with your presence! Let rivers of living waters flow from and thru my life. As I pursue a more intimate relationship with you Father, annihilate the very scent of religion from my life. Amen

"LIGHTS, CAMERA, ACTION"

EXPOSING THE SPOTLIGHT CHRISTIAN

SCRIPTURAL EMPHASIS:

Let your light so shine before men, that they may see your good works, and glorify your Father which in heaven. (Matthew 5:16 KJV)

I want to expose a group of people who thrive off of being in the spotlight. You know the ones that must be seen; the ones that thrive off of being in the fore-front and wouldn't think of ever being in the background. But part of the problem is some of us have created these monsters. We've pampered them, held their hands, rubbed their heads and bandaged their boo-boos. We've fed their egos and filled their heads with so much fluff that they can barely hold it up without our assistance. And why have we done this terrible injustice to them and those who must endure their prideful and pompous attitudes? It's simply because we value their gift more than we value the giver of the gift. And what's even a further injustice to the body of Christ is that we overlook their lifestyles outside of church and justify their sinful deeds and actions by saying, "no one is perfect".

So we continue to allow them to flaunt their gifts and talents in front of the body of Christ because we're afraid if we take them down off of the pedestal "we" built from the ground up, that they will leave the church and take with them the other carnal minded folk who only flock around them just so by some chance some of the spotlight will cast a glimpse of light on them.

I don't understand how one can say they love God and hate their brothers and sisters. I don't understand why these spotlight Christians can be up in front of the body of Christ one minute glorifying God but will walk past their brothers and sisters in Christ and not speak. It's our fault that this is plaguing the Body of Christ. It's our fault because we've created this mess. We've categorized people based upon their gifts and talents, financial status, appearance, and connections. We place them on pedestals to make them feel more important than the one who simply sweeps the church floors.

We place the Preacher so high that he becomes untouchable and unreachable. We place the worship leaders so high that he or she feels like no one else can reach Heaven like he or she can. We treat those with money differently than those who are not as blessed. We pump them up, pat their backs, and pump their egos all for the sake of keeping them happy because we've already calculated their tithes and placed high expectation on the dollar amount of their offering. It's funny how God tells us in His Word not to have respect of person but we do it on a daily basis.

Just in case you don't believe it's in the Bible let's take a look at James 2:1-4 (KJV) *¹My brethren, have not the faith of our Lord Jesus Christ, the Lord of glory, with respect of persons.*

²For if there come unto your assembly a man with a gold ring, in goodly apparel, and there come in also a poor man in vile raiment;

³And ye have respect to him that weareth the gay clothing, and say unto him, Sit thou here in a good place; and say to the poor, Stand thou there, or sit here under my footstool:

⁴Are ye not then partial in yourselves, and are become judges of evil thoughts?

Now let's take an even closer look at this in the Amplified Bible Version:

[1]MY BRETHREN, pay no servile regard to people [show no prejudice, no partiality]. Do not [attempt to] hold and practice the faith of our Lord Jesus Christ [the Lord] of glory [together with snobbery]!

[2]For if a person comes into your congregation whose hands are adorned with gold rings and who is wearing splendid apparel, and also a poor [man] in shabby clothes comes in,

[3]And you pay special attention to the one who wears the splendid clothes and say to him, Sit here in this preferable seat! While you tell the poor [man], stand there! or, Sit there on the floor at my feet!

[4]Are you not discriminating among your own and becoming critics and judges with wrong motives?

This clearly tells us to show no partiality or respect of person. Why then do we practice doing the opposite of what God has instructed us not to do? Are we simply just going to ignore these scriptures? It's absolutely against the nature of Christ to turn our noses up and disregard people because they don't meet our standards.

James 2: 9 tells us if we show respect of person, we have committed sin. Verse 10 of the same chapter is the point I really want to drive home...

[10]For whosoever shall keep the whole law, and yet offend in one point, he is guilty of all.

What is this saying? It's saying regardless of all the other laws you obey; if you offend in one point...if you disobey one law, you become guilty of all. What a price to pay!

This by far is mind-blowing to me...James 1:5 (Amplified):

[5]Listen, my beloved brethren: Has not God chosen those who are poor in the eyes of the world to be rich in faith and in their position as believers and to inherit the kingdom which He has promised to those who love Him?

What a powerful statement! What audacity to turn your nose up to those whom the world looks at as poor and of low degree when through the eyes of God they are rich in faith and in their position as a believer will inherit the kingdom as he promised those who love him. That's enough to make me dance and shout because I may not have a house on the mountaintop, drive in the fanciest car, or have billions of dollars in my bank account, but as long as I walk in obedience, have faith in God, have placed my complete trust in Him, and love Him with all my heart…the kingdom of God will I inherit.

The "spotlight" Christian receives their reward now…with the applause and accolades of men. But those who labor in the vineyard….the "behind the scenes person" will reap a reward far greater than you can imagine. The prayer warrior who labors tirelessly standing in the gap and interceding on behalf of others…their reward will be great. The nursery worker and children's church leader who takes special care of your children; teaching them at an early age to love the Lord and to serve him; great will be their reward. Those who sacrifice their time and families to minister to the incarcerated; great is your reward. But to the one that thrives off the praise of man; who lives to be patted on the back and receive standing ovations; you've already received your reward.

A Christian should never desire to please man but to please God. A Christian should never seek man for attention, but to seek the attention of God. Your thought process should be, "What can I do to get God's attention?" What can I do to be pleasing in the sight of God? Never should you seek the approval of man. Have you forgotten who created man? Don't get caught up in the creation but in the Creator. Great is your reward when you turn your attention on pleasing God. The Bible tells us to "be not weary in well doing, for in due season we shall reap if we faint not." (Galatians 6:9)

It's time to stop placing those with titles and positions on a higher scale than others. In the sight of God it doesn't matter if you're the Janitor or the Bishop. God is looking at the motives and intent of your heart. Why do you do what you do? Is it to garner the acceptance of man or is it to be pleasing in the sight of God? Is it to build your kingdom or God's kingdom? God desires pure servitude and the greatest example of that is our Lord and Savior Jesus Christ.

PRAYER OF EMPOWERMENT:

Father, forgive us for being more concerned with what man thinks about us than what you think about us. Forgive us for tainting the gifts and talents you've blessed us with by using them for our own glory. Forgive us for prostituting ourselves for the sake of attention, applause and accolades. Teach us to be true servants. Teach us to walk circumspectly and to do all things decently and in order for your glory. Empower us to train the generation before us to use their gifts and talents for your glory and yours alone. Amen

"TWO FACED"

Which side are you on?

SCRIPTURAL EMPHASIS:

A double minded man is unstable in all his ways. (James 1:8 KJV)

A double minded man is one who is tossed to and fro by every wind and doctrine. A double minded man can also be viewed and labeled as a hypocrite. He's one way today and then on tomorrow he's someone different. On Sunday this person can be seen praising and worshipping God, but as soon as Monday rolls in this same person is seen doing everything contrary to his public display of worship on Sunday. The double minded man can be deemed as spiritually bi-polar; consistently wavering; torn between two opinions; saying one thing but doing the total opposite.

Come close to God and He will come close to you. [Recognize that you are] sinners, get your soiled hands clean; [realize that you have been disloyal] wavering individuals with divided interests, and purify your hearts [of your spiritual adultery]. (James 4:8 Amplified)

We again see in the scriptures that a double minded man is very unstable. This person has divided interests; they are disloyal; committing spiritual adultery. What a powerful description! Let's take a look at this....Spiritual Adultery is not based upon female – male sexual relationships, but it has everything to do

with Christ – Man relationship and/or fellowship. We, the
church are called the Bride of Christ. When we accept Christ as
our Lord and Savior we have committed our lives to Him. We
are married to Christ. The scriptures are very clear about
spiritual adultery.

*You [are like] unfaithful wives [having illicit love affairs with the
world and breaking your marriage vow to God]! Do you not know
that being the world's friend is being God's enemy? So whoever
chooses to be a friend of the world takes his stand as an enemy of
God.*

*[5]Or do you suppose that the Scripture is speaking to no purpose that
says, The Spirit Whom He has caused to dwell in us yearns over us
and He yearns for the Spirit [to be welcome] with a jealous love?
(James 4:4-5)*

You simply cannot love God and love the world at the same time.
You must choose one or the other. You can't pick out the parts
you want of God and then pick out the parts you want from the
world. You cannot serve two masters. Running after the lasts
fads and popular trends should be avoided. The word of God
uses sexual implications to show us how He longs for us. We are
His Bride. In the natural sense a Bride longs for her husband;
she seeks to please him and love him unconditionally. The same
is with our Lord and Savior; He loves us. He longs to show us
His love and feel our love in return. He doesn't desire that we
embrace the things of the world. Our desire should be to live for
Him and to please Him only; for our God is a jealous God and
we belong to Him. When we allow the things of the world to
infiltrate our lives, we in essence are cheating on God. Our will
must align with His will…not only His permissive will but His
perfect will. When we subject our spirit man to the things of the
world we become weak. Our strength is depleted.

*How weak and spent with longing and lust is your heart and mind,
says the Lord God, seeing you do all these things, the work of a bold,
domineering harlot, [31]In that you build your vaulted place (brothel)*

at the head of every street and make your high place at every crossing. But you were not like a harlot because you scorned pay.

For long ago [in Egypt] I broke your yoke and burst your bonds [not that you might be free, but that you might serve Me] and long ago you shattered the yoke and snapped the bonds [of My law which I put upon you]; you said, I will not serve and obey You! For upon every high hill and under every green tree you [eagerly] prostrated yourself [in idolatrous worship], playing the harlot.

Let's take a look further into Jeremiah 2:20. God destroyed the yoke of bondage so that we can be free to serve Him, but because of our infidelity and our unfaithfulness we chose rather to lay down wherever we could find a place to lay our head in idolatrous worship; being strum along like a fiddle; manipulated by the enemy to do his evil works. We became nothing more than a prostitute; going along with whatever tickles our fancy or makes us feel good. Instead of being a committed servant of God, we traded in our freedom to become a slave to the devil. What foolishness!

What's even further unfortunate and sad is that some say they want the best of both worlds. In one breath, "I love the Lord", in the next they're reciting the latest secular hip hop lyrics. In one instance they stand before the people of God offering up what they deem to be pure worship; in the next instance they're outside of the sanctuary lighting up a cigarette or talking about their sinful exploits the night before. Double minded!

Their heart is divided. They wear a two-faced mask. Part of the problem is people think they can do what they want to do and live how they want to live. They believe the power is in their hands and they can do whatever they please to do on their own. They don't see that they really need God. They look at their accomplishments and successes. They look at all they've acquired; money, cars, homes and jewels; they feel they have

everything they need; they believe they have it going on. But my Bible reads in the book of Hosea that Israel felt the same way, but let's take a look at what happened.

Israel was once a lush vine, bountiful in grapes. The more lavish the harvest, the more promiscuous the worship. The more money they got, the more they squandered on gods-in-their-own-image. Their sweet smiles are sheer lies. They're guilty as sin. God will smash their worship shrines, pulverize their god-images. (Hosea 10:1-2)

They too thought they had it all. The more they attained, the more they turned away from God. Their worship became tainted and instead of worshipping the true and living God they turned to become worshippers and lovers of themselves. It became a show; look what I've accomplished; look what I have; look at the car I drive and the house I live in. I did this; I acquired all of this. They pushed God aside; treating Him as if he's a street hustler. The only time they cried out to Him is when they found themselves in trouble. When their earthly treasures were no longer flourishing they then want to run to God for help. Double minded! Two faced! Backstabbers! Liars and cheaters!

And Elijah came unto all the people, and said, how long halt ye between two opinions? If the LORD be God, follow him: but if Baal, then follow him. And the people answered him not a word. (1 Kings 18:21)

I believe those who operate with a double mind truly desire to serve the Lord, but they are so drawn to the façade of the world that they become unable to resist the temptations and pleasures of the world. The word however is very clear; no man can serve two masters.

Now I want to delve into an issue that many notice, but will not confront. There are Leaders, Pastors, Preachers, Teachers, Evangelist and so on that will be held accountable for the diluted word that is being taught and preached in churches all across the nation. They stand before souls in desperate need of a true word from God. What happened to sermons on Holiness? What has happened to sermons on the consequences of sin? Where are the teachings on living a victorious life? Nowadays it's all about appeasing people. Leaders don't want to upset or anger their members. They have become more concerned with acquiring million dollar edifices, popularity and fame. They choose not to rock the boat because they don't want their numbers to be affected; so instead they preach a dissected and most time disease infected sermon. They preach and teach emotional and dramatic messages about absolutely nothing at all to entice the people to return. They inject the church with hype and not hope; greed and not gratitude; fluff and not faith.

The days of denouncing sin has become a thing of old. They don't preach biblical standards. They no longer teach about the wages of sin being death. Teaching on holiness has all but vanished from the church; they say holiness is outdated; it no longer applies to today's church. It's a new day. We have to meet the people where they are; getting on their level. Instead of the sinner being lead to Christ; the church is being drawn and lead to the world. I've never seen so many carnal minded leaders in my life. They go along with everything; every wind and doctrine is fine with them. They don't care if secular music is played in the house of God. They promote having their young people center stage "shaking what their mama's gave them"; bodies gyrating and flesh on display. Youth ministries have become nothing more than a night club. There's no difference with what goes on in the club with what is allowed in some churches.

Carnality has taken over the church, and no one wants to take a radical stand. It's a tragedy when you can't tell a saint from a sinner. The so called saints are cursing people out, drinking, smoking, clubbing, fornicating, and participating in lewd and lascivious sexual acts. What's happened to the standard? God told us to be HOLY! Holiness is a lifestyle. We serve a HOLY God, and we have been commanded to be HOLY.

We are living in perilous times. It's time out for this carefree mentality about living saved. It's time out for putting on your mask of salvation on Sunday, but before service ends you've flipped the mask over and blended in with the world. We are to be separate from the world. We live in this world, but we are not of this world.

Wherefore come out from among them, and be ye separate, saith the Lord, and touch not the unclean thing; and I will receive you. (2 Corinthians 6:17 KJV)

You cannot seriously expect anything from God if your temple is defiled. We are to refrain from anything unclean. Our bodies are the temple of the Holy Ghost.

Know ye not that ye are the temple of God, and that the Spirit of God dwelleth in you? [17]If any man defile the temple of God, him shall God destroy; for the temple of God is holy, which temple ye are.

People of God, it's time that we get our focus back. It's time to renew our minds in the word of God. We cannot sit back with our mouths closed and are hands neatly folded in our laps doing nothing. It's not enough to just talk about what's wrong in the body of Christ, but it's time to do something about it. It's time to cry aloud and spare not. It's time to lift up our voices like a trumpet and reveal to those who transgress the error of their way. (Isaiah 58:1 paraphrased)

We do not serve a schizophrenic God. God is not double minded. He's the same yesterday, today and forever more. It's time to get our minds right and stand up for the Kingdom of God and take back our rightful place. We must take the Kingdom by force.

And from the days of John the Baptist until now the kingdom of heaven suffereth violence, and the violent take it by force. (Matthew 11:12 KJV)

PRAYER OF EMPOWERMENT:

Father, forgive us for our double minded ways. Forgive us for wavering in the faith. Forgive us for living a lie. Forgive us God and remove the double sided masks that we wear. Teach us to live holy. Give us the strength and the fortitude to stand up and take our rightful place in the Kingdom. Help us to rightly divide the word of truth; preaching and teaching only what your word says. Empower us to regain our focus and put on the mind of Christ that we may be fruitful in your Kingdom. Prepare us to cry aloud and spare not; revealing to men and women all across the nation that the wages of sin is death but the gift of God is eternal life. Let us not waiver in our belief, but let us rise up with a renewed mind and a transformed lifestyle and to the work you have called and commissioned us to do. Thank you for being a God full of grace and mercy. Lord in these last and evil days, show yourself strong to your people. Help us to not only have a form of godliness; yet denying the power. Let our desire be to continually walk according to your ways. Amen

ARE YOU IN IT?

SCRIPTURAL EMPHASIS:

³ **Oh, that we might know the LORD! Let us press on to know him.**
  He will respond to us as surely as the arrival of dawn or the coming of rains in early spring." (Hosea 6:3 NLT)

I've often heard people say they are "sold out" for Christ. But what does that statement truly mean? In my opinion, it's that point in your life where you know that you will do anything to please God…that you will put aside self to follow His will and His way. It's when the plans that you have for your life become the plans that God predestined for you since before the beginning of time. It's being able to look in the mirror and see "YOUR" faults and "YOUR" frailties and then having enough courage to face them head on and ask God to help you overcome them.

So many people say they are "Christians". They use the title of being a Christian as an everyday saying or slogan, but fail to delve into the true meaning of Christianity. When asked, their eager to say yes I'm a Christian. But it's mere words on tainted and flawed lips. It's sad but in today's society the title, "Christian" has become as ordinary as Charmin toilet paper, and that's exactly how we treat it. We unravel it, wipe up our mess (justify it) and flush it down the toilet (dismiss it). I tire easy of people who profess the name of Christ as their Lord and Savior, yet they bear no fruit.

Might I dare add that those who say they carry the name of Jesus in their hearts, who confess of their sins daily (because daily we sin) and have invited Christ to dwell on the inside of them, are not perfect creatures. For the bible says in Romans 3:23, "For all have sinned, and come short of the glory of God." We "All" have something in our lives that we need to rid ourselves of and be delivered from. There are no "perfect" Christians, but we are to strive daily for perfection and spiritual excellence in Christ; disciplining ourselves to not just be hearers of the Word but doers of the Word also. We ought not to preach the Word to others unless we are first partakers of the Word and we are living what the Word of God says. So I ask the question, Are you truly in it or are you just merely around it? Are you in it just long enough to get a prayer answered or do you remain in it when you can't seem to hear the voice of God? Are you truly in it because you want God to create in you a clean heart and renew in you a right spirit?

Are you just merely hanging around it, acting like you're in it, but the first sign of trouble you're denouncing that you even know Christ....or let's hit closer to home...you gossip, back-bite, lie, and cheat yet profess that you love the Lord. You stand in judgment of others, picking out their faults and frailties all the while overlooking the sin ridden billboard sign plastered on your forehead?

Why do we waste time saying we're Christians, when we talk about our brothers and sisters. We examine everyone else but we fail to ever turn the microscope on ourselves. We sit back and diagnose everyone...oh he's an adulterer, she's a liar, she's a backbiter, he's a whore monger, he's a homosexual....But we fail to examine our own lives, motives and intent. We fail to look inward and see the ugly side of ourselves. We want everyone to believe that we sit on the right hand of the Father. It's rather disturbing how we title ourselves Christians, but do not want to live as Christ has instructed us to live. It's more to being a Christian than just saying you're one....You must live the life you claim to represent. Are you in it or just merely around it?

Are you truly "Sold Out" for Christ? Have you truly dismissed from your life "EVERYTHING" that is not like Christ? Do you truly want to do nothing but please God? It's time to examine our hearts and get to the place where God wants us...IN HIM and not merely hanging "around" Him. We should desire a deeper and more intimate relationship with our Lord and Savior. It should be our sincere prayer that our lives are an example that will represent well our Lord and Savior. Realizing that we are not perfect and that we will make mistakes and may even fall along the way, but we should yet strive to be all that we can be in Christ, not just professing to be a Christian, but actually striving daily to being one.

PRAYER OF EMPOWERMENT:

Father, as I stand before you seeking your face, reveal to me whatever it is about me that is not pleasing to you. Lord, show me, ME! Give me the courage to look in the spiritual mirror and be strong enough to handle what I find staring back at me. Lord, mold and make me; fix and change me. Examine my heart Lord, and if you find anything that should not be, I ask that you would remove it. My desire is to be like you. I don't want to misrepresent you by merely saying I'm a Christian, but I want to live the life. Examine my motives and intent and let them be pure; bringing glory to you and you alone. Empower me to be a God pleaser. Lord I desire that you take up residence within me. I desire to be holy as you are holy. I want to know you intimately and not just know of you. Empower me to stand in right relationship with you. Amen

"TWISTED"

Scriptural Emphasis: St. Luke 13:10-17

Focal Scripture: St. Luke 13:13

Then he put his hands on her, and immediately she straightened up and praised God.

Churches of today have lost its zeal, and have become weak and fragile. Satan literally has placed a choke hold on the body of Christ. The enemy has lured believers into bondage by painting a flattering canvas full of fame, fortune, materialism and commercialism. The church has moved from winning souls to Christ; and has moved into filling seats to obtain mega status. No longer is sound doctrine taught, but now it's all about "feel good" messages that excite the congregants, but does not add depth to their relationship with God.

The church is bowed over; crippled; twisted; broken. It has lost some if not all of its power, effectiveness, strength, and fortitude to endure adversity. For years the church has been in a downward spiral; leaving the presence of God to attain the acceptance of worldly men. The church has begun adopting the mindset and rules of the world; leaving the soundness of the word of God. The church has twisted the word of God for ill gain and profit. It's become a cesspool of pride and arrogance. Preachers standing behind the podium preaching only what will get an emotional rise out of the body of believers and leaving unspoken the word that pricks the heart with conviction. It's a terrible injustice to the body of Christ. Its crippling effects are astounding.

The enemy has blinded leadership; which now result in blind Shepherds leading blind sheep. They spew ignorance and foolishness over the pulpit trying to sway believers from what the word of God says. They are now indoctrinating people into believing anything goes. They want you to believe that repentance is a thing of old and is no longer required.

The lamps once trimmed and burning is now dimly lit or not lit at all. The truth is being twisted to appease man. Instead of subduing the enemy; the body of Christ is now being subdued and silenced. The church is sick and no one is reaching out for the hand of God to seek healing and deliverance.

Did we forget that we are the church; the Bride of Christ? Did we forget that Christ is coming to unite with and take his Bride home?

Revelation 19:6-8 (KJV)

[6] And I heard as it were the voice of a great multitude, and as the voice of many waters, and as the voice of mighty thunderings, saying, Alleluia: for the Lord God omnipotent reigneth.

[7] Let us be glad and rejoice, and give honour to him: for the marriage of the Lamb is come, and his wife hath made herself ready.

[8] And to her was granted that she should be arrayed in fine linen, clean and white: for the fine linen is the righteousness of saints.

We have clear instruction on how to prepare for the Lord's return. As He gives an illustration of how a husband should love his wife; he also relates it to His love for His Bride (the Church).

Ephesians 5:25-27 (King James Version)

²⁵Husbands love your wives, even as Christ also loved the church, and gave himself for it;

²⁶That he might sanctify and cleanse it with the washing of water by the word,

²⁷That he might present it to himself a glorious church, not having spot, or wrinkle, or any such thing; but that it should be holy and without blemish.

The condition of the church is far from this description. The church has become tainted with the world and the things of the world. But there is an answer…Repentance. The church must repent of its unlawful ways and return to God. If repentance does not take place many will fall away and die in their sins. God is waiting to lay His hands on the Body of Christ, but the body must repent. The words says in, 2 Chronicles 7:14 (King James Version)

¹⁴If my people, which are called by my name, shall humble themselves, and pray, and seek my face, and turn from their wicked ways; then will I hear from heaven, and will forgive their sin, and will heal their land.

Until the body of Christ repents and turns from the wickedness of this world it will continue on its downward spiral. But when the Body of Christ takes a stand, repent and return to the Lord; that is when God will hear our cry, forgive our sins and heal our land. Just as the woman infirmed for eighteen years was immediately healed once God laid his hands on her; so shall the church; the Body of Christ be immediately healed, restored and strengthened once it repents.

PRAYER OF EMPOWERMENT:

Father, forgive us for desecrating your body. Forgive us for allowing the world to take up residence within us. Forgive us for yielding to tainted sermons and unlawful deeds. Lord hear our cries, forgive us, heal us, strengthen us; make our crooked places straight. Saturate the dry places in our lives. Let us return to our first love; living a lifestyle of holiness. Forgive us for allowing ourselves to become indoctrinated with the mindset and rules of this world; allowing the enemy full reign in our sanctuaries, homes, and lives. Heal our land God, deliver us from the hand of the enemy, strengthen us to rise up and proclaim that you are a holy God and we are to be a holy people. Return us to our rightful place…letting your righteousness shine within us for the lost to be drawn to your light. Amen

"IT STILL TAKES IT"

SCRIPTURAL EMPHASIS:

Proverbs 3:1-2 (KJV)

[1]**My son, forget not my law; but let thine heart keep my commandments:** [2]**For length of days, and long life, and peace, shall they add to thee.**

One morning as I was driving to work the Lord put in my spirit, "What it took is what it takes". As I thought about this topic, it took me back to the days of the old church. It took me back to the times where repentance was heavily taught. It took me back to the Friday night prayer and tarry services; where you'd lay on the altar before God crying out to him; asking for forgiveness; asking to be set free and delivered from the snares and bondage of the enemy. I was reminded of what God expects from His children....that we should seek His face not just when things are going well, but every single day should be a day of seeking God and the things of God. But what happens is we get comfortable because everything is going well and we stop doing what it took to get us where we are; failing to realize that what it took; it still takes.

God doesn't want a part-time lover. He wants a full time, lifetime commitment. So today God is saying, "Return to Me, your first love!" Regardless of your current situation, your faults and failures; regardless of your test, trials and tribulations...RETURN TO ME. For, He said in His word that He would never leave or forsake us; nor leave our seed begging bread. God wants that same commitment from us. Today God has spoken a mandate for us to return to our first love. We are to be unwavering in the faith. We are to trust Him completely. We are to forsake our ways for His ways. We are to deny ourselves, take up the cross and follow him. Our daily testimony should be, "Lord I'm chasing after you, no matter what I have to do because I need you more and more. It's time to stop playing Russian roulette with our lives. It's too late to be straddling the fence; having one foot in and one foot out. It's time to stop playing with the fire of sin because eventually you will get burned. It's time for us to forsake all others...to let go of everything and everyone that is not of God. It's time to get real about the "real" God we serve.

Time is drawing near, and his return is surely upon us. The word of God tells us if we draw nigh to God, He'll draw nigh to us. If we instead of being men chasers and men pleasers would dedicate our lives to being a God chaser and a God pleaser, there would be no good withheld from us. What it took then is still what it takes now.

Some contemporary Christians will try and persuade you that it doesn't take all of that to live for Christ. I beg to differ. It takes all that and more. The enemy is out to destroy the people of God and it is imperative that we become radical about our walk with Christ. We as children of God need to adopt the saying, "For God I live and for God I die" We have to become super radical about our Lord and Savior. God is waiting with arms open wide ready for us to return to Him. He's waiting for us to give him our undivided attention. God has so much for the people of God but we forfeit our blessing every time we take our eyes off of

Him. If we would only forsake our will and our ways and walk in the perfect will of God, we would be blessed beyond measure. If only we would forsake our selfish desires and carnal thinking, we would impact the nations and draw the lost to Christ by the droves. We can only do this if we sincerely and genuinely return to our rightful place in God. It's decision time! Do we continue to live beneath our privilege? Or do we rise up, empower ourselves with the word of God and commit our lives to God completely?

What it took then, it takes now! Don't allow the enemy to confuse your mind into thinking you can live any kind of way and still obtain kingdom status. Have you forgotten who the devil is? He's the father of lies and there is no truth found in him. Don't think for one second that you can live a hellish lifestyle and obtain the crown of life. God has given us a blueprint by which we should live and it's a lifestyle of holiness. There should never be any type of compromise when it comes to serving God. Either you're for Him or against Him. The word of God gives us clear instructions on how kingdom people should live He has no desire that anyone should perish, but that all should walk in the knowledge of God and be saved. The word of God tells us in 2 Peter 3:14 (NIV) that we should make every effort to be found spotless, blameless and at peace with Him. Why? Because the Day of Judgment is near.

Be careful people of God that as 2 Peter 3:17 declares, we are to be on guard so that we will not be carried away by the error of lawless men and fall from your secure place. There are those that will try and convince you that the Bible is not to be taken literally. That it's just a book of old stories and traditions that we do not have to abide by, but on the contrary; we are to abide by every word written. The bible is our map...our compass to eternal life. It will lead us down the path of truth and righteousness. It will reveal to us traps and snares that the enemy has set. We are to apply the principles found in the word of God to our everyday lives. The word of God is defined in Psalms 119:105 as a lamp unto our feet and a light unto our path. When we consume the word, every place our feet tread upon is illuminated. When walking in a dark land, the word on the inside of us will shine forth light not just for our benefit but to draw others to the light...the light of Jesus Christ.

What it took back then; it takes now! It takes you to enter your prayer closets laying before God in humble submission. It takes pushing back the plate; denying our flesh just to get closer to God. It takes cutting certain people from our lives that are not living a lifestyle conducive to holiness. It takes sometimes in the midnight hour falling on your knees interceding on behalf of someone else. Sometimes you have to turn your television off and unplug the phone; shutting out the cares of the world and halting our busy schedules.

It takes assembling yourselves together with other believers; worshipping and praising the only true and living God. It takes putting the latest gossip magazine or the latest romance novel down; replacing them with the word of God. Yes, people of God it takes this and so much more. Stop allowing the devil to make mockery of your walk with Christ. You may lose people along the way, but if that's what it takes to see Jesus in the end...Do it. It's time to get radical in our worship; radical in our praise. It's time for the people of God to stand up and stop taking a back seat to the enemy. We are more than conquerors. The victory already belongs to us. Stop living beneath your privilege and start doing whatever it takes to secure hearing the Lord say, Well done, good and faithful servant; thou hast been faithful over a few things, I will make thee ruler over many things: enter thou into the joy of thy lord. (Matthew 25:23 KJV)

The passages of scripture below describe what will occur on that great day. Be ye also ready. It's now time to pursue God with Pit Bull tenacity. Let everyday be a day of preparation; because the Lord's return is imminent.

2 Peter 3:8-20 (New International Version)

[8]*But do not forget this one thing, dear friends: with the Lord a day is like a thousand years, and a thousand years are like a day.* [9]*The Lord is not slow in keeping his promise, as some understand slowness. He is patient with you, not wanting anyone to perish, but everyone to come to repentance.*

[10]*But the day of the Lord will come like a thief. The heavens will disappear with a roar; the elements will be destroyed by fire, and the earth and everything in it will be laid bare.*

[11]*Since everything will be destroyed in this way, what kind of people ought you to be? You ought to live holy and godly lives* [12]*as you look forward to the day of God and speed its coming. That day will bring about the destruction of the heavens by fire, and the elements will melt in the heat.* [13]*But in keeping with his promise we are looking forward to a new heaven and a new earth, the home of righteousness.*

[14]*So then, dear friends, since you are looking forward to this, make every effort to be found spotless, blameless and at peace with him.* [15]*Bear in mind that our Lord's patience means salvation, just as our dear brother Paul also wrote you with the wisdom that God gave him.* [16]*He writes the same way in all his letters, speaking in them of these matters. His letters contain some things that are hard to understand, which ignorant and unstable people distort, as they do the other Scriptures, to their own destruction.*

[17]*Therefore, dear friends, since you already know this, be on your guard so that you may not be carried away by the error of lawless men and fall from your secure position.* [18]*But grow in the grace and*

knowledge of our Lord and Savior Jesus Christ. To him be glory both now and forever! Amen

PRAYER OF EMPOWERMENT:

Father, empower us to keep your law and forget not your commandments. Lord let the people of God return to you...our first love. Let us continue to be on guard so that we will not be carried away by the error of lawless men and fall from our secure place in you. Let us remain sober and vigilant in order to detect the enemy's tactics, plots and schemes. Lord, empower us to make every effort to be found spotless, blameless and at peace with you. Remove carnal thinking and negative speaking from our lives and replace it with words of life, encouragement and hope. Let our lives be a mirrored reflection of you. Amen.

PEARLS OF PATIENCE & ENDURANCE

THE PROFITABILITY OF DISCOMFORT

SCRIPTURAL EMPHASIS:

For our light affliction, which is but for a moment, worketh for us a far more exceeding and eternal weight of glory. 2 Corinthians 4:17

Some times in life we go through a season of discomfort; where things just don't feel too good. We often question why we are going through so much and when it will cease. Trouble is found all around us. Some have lost their jobs and only means of financial support. Home foreclosures are steadily increasing. Banks going under, businesses shutting their doors. Sickness is rampant in the land. Deaths, divorce, and destruction is beating down our front doors. Some are robbing Peter to pay Paul just to make ends meet. We've become inundated with uncomfortable situations. It feels like a pair of shoes that is 2 sizes too small cutting off the blood supply in our feet until they go completely numb. It's overwhelming to say the least. The cares of life at times seem to sneak up on us and try to choke life from us. We begin to question God and then give our list of bullet points of why WE shouldn't have to endure these things.

- I'm a faithful tither and giver.
- I pray without ceasing.
- I work tirelessly in the church I attend.

- I feed the hungry, clothe the naked, and provide shelter to the homeless.
- I don't drink or smoke
- I don't indulge in profane things.
- I fast regularly.

And so on, and so on, and so on......

What we fail to realize is God already knows these things about us. God knows us better than we know ourselves. We all have imperfections, blemishes and weaknesses that must be destroyed from our lives. So He puts us in the fire to burn off the very things we think are insignificant issues, but they are actually destroying us. You know, the occasional "white" lie we tell; the way we turn our nose up to those less fortunate than we are; the way we talk about the flaws we see in others; you know, the way we minimize our flaws by maximizing the flaws in others. He sees the times when we backbite and gossip; the times where we talk about one another, even those we deem to call "FRIEND". He sees the knife in our hand plunging toward the back of the one we dislike. He sees how we use our tongue to manipulate and tear down our brothers and sisters.

He knows the secret hate, envy and jealousy we harbor in our hearts. He watches as we make our "stuff" our gods, puffing out our chests as if we have attained all because we have a few dollars in the bank.

These are the very things we try to overlook as we stand pious and proud proclaiming we are a child of God. These are the things God is trying to purge us from. It becomes necessary to throw us in the fire so we can remain pure before him. It may not feel good to us, but it's definitely for our good. We can't be effective in ministry or in life until we've been refined in the fire. The bible tells us clearly that we must lay aside every weight and sin that easily beset (trouble or harass) us.

I like how the Amplified version puts it: Hebrews
12:1 (Amplified Bible)

 Therefore then, since we are surrounded by so great a cloud of
witnesses [who have borne testimony to the Truth], let us strip
off and throw aside every encumbrance (unnecessary weight)
and that sin which so readily (deftly and cleverly) clings to and
entangles us, and let us run with patient endurance and steady
and active persistence the appointed course of the race that is set
before us. For in the end we will find that the discomforts of life
have now become profitable. When we go through the fire and
allow the Refiner to burn away everything that is not like HIM,
we will come out as pure gold. We will then be able to go forth
and effectively promote and build the Kingdom of God. And
remember where there is no "TEST" there is no
"TESTIMONY". Let God turn your Pressure into Praise.
In conclusion meditate once again on this scripture:

2 Corinthians 4:17
For our light affliction, which is but for a moment, worketh for
us a far more exceeding and eternal weight of glory.

PRAYER OF EMPOWERMENT:

Father, empower me to accept my test and trials and help me to
go through them with a praise on my lips and with a spirit of
worship. I decree and declare that with each test and trial, I am
made stronger, wiser and better. Lord, burn off anything that is
not like you. Refine me in the fire so my life will be a testament
of your saving grace and your delivering power. Thank you for
showing me that where there is no test…there is no testimony.
My pressure will transform into praise. Amen

"The Art of War"

SCRIPTURAL EMPHASIS:

For though we walk in the flesh, we do not war after the flesh: (For the weapons of our warfare are not carnal, but mighty through God to the pulling down of strong holds ;) Corinthians 10:3-4 (KJV)

The above referenced scripture assures us that though we walk (live) in the flesh we are not fighting in warfare according to our flesh and we do not use human weapons, because the weapons of our warfare are not of the physical nature, but they are mighty through God to destroy strongholds. The Message version of the bible puts it like this:

The world is unprincipled. It's dog-eat-dog out there! The world doesn't fight fair. But we don't live or fight our battles that way—never have and never will. The tools of our trade aren't for marketing or manipulation, but they are for demolishing that entire massively corrupt culture. We use our powerful God-tools for smashing warped philosophies, tearing down barriers erected against the truth of God, fitting every loose thought and emotion and impulse into the structure of life shaped by Christ. Our tools are ready at hand for clearing the ground of every obstruction and building lives of obedience into maturity.

The world would have us operate in an unprincipled way. The world would have us fight flesh with our flesh; tooth and nail; shedding blood. But that's not the way God intended for His people. The world uses the art of manipulation which is a form of witchcraft. The world operates in getting you to think the way it thinks in order to control your every thought and action. It's like being a puppet on a string. When the world wants you to go right it pulls that string and you do exactly what the world dictates.

But spiritual warfare is totally opposite of the world's views and standards. Let's take a look at the word "warfare"....I found this word to be very interesting. We know that war means a struggle or competition between opposing forces or for a particular end. Fare means a range of food; it also means the price charged to transport a person.

Let's delve into this deeper.

If we look at this from the spiritual standpoint using the first definition of fare....a range of food; we can assume that being in spiritual warfare you must eat the right stuff in order to build up your resistance against the enemy. How do we build up our resistance toward the enemy? By feeding our spirit man the Word of God. We must not only read and study the Word of God but we must also chew and digest it which will make us stronger in Christ and it will enable us to withstand the wiles of the devil. Just as we eat natural foods to strengthen the natural man which builds up our resistance against sickness, we must also feed our spirit man to fight against and resist the temptations of the enemy.

The Bible says in Ephesians 6:13-17:

[13] *Wherefore take unto you the whole armor of God, that ye may be able to withstand in the evil day, and having done all, to stand.*

[14] *Stand therefore, having your loins girt about with truth, and having on the breastplate of righteousness;*

[15] *And your feet shod with the preparation of the gospel of peace;*

^{16}Above all, taking the shield of faith, wherewith ye shall be able to quench all the fiery darts of the wicked.

^{17}And take the helmet of salvation, and the sword of the Spirit, which is the word of God:

Now let's look at the second definition of "fare".... the price charged to transport a person.

This really ignited a fire within me...because when looking at this with my spiritual eyes it shows me that in spiritual warfare there's a price that must be paid in order to be transported or moved to the destination God has ordained. So in order for me to get where I'm going I must first offer up a sacrifice, which takes me back to the first definition of a range of food. In order for me to go from battle to victory there's some things I must do first. I first have to ensure I'm battle ready by consuming and immersing myself in the Word of God. Remember, we're not fighting flesh and blood, but we're fighting against principalities, against powers, against the rulers of darkness of this world, against spiritual wickedness in high places. (Ephesians 6:12)

So we must spiritually prepare for spiritual warfare. Let's break down the tools we will need in order to be transported from war to victory:

First, we will need to "Stand" having our "loins girt about with truth". Well what does that mean? It means we must equip and surround ourselves with truth...Truth being the Word of God.

Next, we will need to ensure we have on the "breastplate of righteousness". The breastplate represents defensive armor. Righteousness signifies spiritual integrity and being correct in judgment.

Once we have on the "breastplate of righteousness" we must ensure our "feet our shod with the preparation of the gospel of peace." We must face the enemy with firm footed stability,

promptness, and the readiness to produce the goodness of the Gospel of peace.

Above all, we must then take the "shield of faith" which will cover you from whatever the enemy throws your way in attack and quench the fiery darts of the wicked.

Finally we must take the "helmet of Salvation" and the Sword of the Spirit" which is the Word of God. We must put on Salvation to cover us and carry the sword of the spirit to defend and fight for us.

Don't spend time fighting with physical hands, but learn to trust God and fight against the enemy in the spirit realm. How do we fight against the enemy? We must first and foremost, live a life of obedience to God. We must be completely and totally sold out for Christ. We must also have a matured prayer life. Prayer is the vehicle that takes our petitions to the Lord who in turn takes our petitions and returns them with resolve attached to them. It's futile and useless to argue and debate with the enemy. The Bible tells us if we hold our peace, He will fight our battles.

Secondly, we must have a strong and mature prayer life. It's important that we daily communicate with the Lord. Maturity in prayer is essential in combating the tactics of the enemy. Prayer strengthens our relationship with Christ. Prayer enables us to walk in the hope of God's word and live a victorious life.

Thirdly, we must have the heart of God. We must be men and women after God's own heart. We must strive to please God daily. To have the heart of God requires us to spend quality time with God. We must study the word of God, practice and apply it. Having the heart of God requires us to denounce anything that is not like or of God. We must have a passionate love for God. Mark 12:30 says, And thou shalt love the Lord thy God with all thy heart, and with all thy soul, and with all thy mind, and with all thy strength: this is the first commandment.

We will all be faced with tests, trials and temptations, but we must ensure that as we face the issues of life that we are fully equipped and ready for battle.

Prayer of Empowerment:

Father, as you go before us to prepare the way; equip us to be ready for the battle. Empower us to overcome the enemy by filling us with your Word. Give us strength to stand through the heat of the battle, and when we feel like the enemy is at our heels and defeat is imminent, empower us to not retreat but to Stand even the more on the truth of your word; for in the end we win if we don't give in. Amen.

"LET GOD BE GOD"

SCRIPTURAL EMPHASIS:

[7-9] Just after that, Hanani the seer came to Asa king of Judah and said, "Because you went for help to the king of Aram and didn't ask GOD for help, you've lost a victory over the army of the king of Aram. Didn't the Ethiopians and Libyans come against you with superior forces, completely outclassing you with their chariots and cavalry? But you asked GOD for help and he gave you the victory. GOD is always on the alert, constantly on the lookout for people who are totally committed to him. You were foolish to go for human help when you could have had God's help. Now you're in trouble—one round of war after another." (2 Chronicles 16:9 Message)

I dare to believe that one thing that angers God is when we pray asking Him for help and instead of allowing Him to work on our behalf, we put our hands in it or ask man to assist. There is no need asking God to fix it, if you're going to try and fix it yourself. We go to God daily petitioning Him for this or that, and daily we find ourselves becoming too impatient to simply trust His power, ability and authority to wait for Him to move on our behalf. Why pray if you're going to worry? Why ask God to handle something for you if you're going to try and handle it on your own?

What baffles me even more is that we know that God has "all" power and authority. We know that God can do anything but fail. We know that God is a strong deliverer; a mighty fortress. We know that God has overcome the world. So why do we continue to pursue things on our own? When we do this we in essence tell God we don't need Him. Instead of letting God be God, we make ourselves into little gods trying to fix what we have no power or ability to fix. We bind the hands of God when we get involved and in the way. Step back, sit down and let God be God in your life.

Don't call on Him to move on your behalf if you're going to try and fix it yourself. Don't pray and ask God for a miracle if you're going to orchestrate your own. When we ask God to work on our behalf it's not for us to get the glory but that He will get the glory. Too many times we want the glory, applause and accolades to be showered on us. We want others to see what we've done so they can give us the praise. God is not pleased with this type of attitude. Our daily walk with Christ should always be motivated by God getting the glory out of our lives.

If we say we believe that God is able to do exceedingly abundantly above anything we ask or think, we then need to take our hands off the situation and allow God to be God. I believe that many who say they trust God really don't trust God at all. They are bound by what they see only. If they don't see it then in their eyes it doesn't exist. But the bible clearly tells us that our walk should be that of faith and not based upon sight.

For we walk by faith, not by sight. (2 Corinthians 5:7)

You must know that God is God. If God said it, He will do just what he says. But we would rather put our trust in man; knowing full well that man will fail us every time, but God is incapable of failing us. So why do we put our trust in man? Is it

163

because we can physically see man? Again, we walk by faith and not by sight. Just because you see it does not mean it is so. The enemy has many deceptive vices and he always begins with planting seeds of deception in the mind. The enemy has a way of making you see things that really do not exist. He will paint a pretty picture to captivate your senses but all the while he's deceiving you. Satan plays on our emotions. Once he has control of your mind he has control of your life. Within man no good thing resides.

And I know that nothing good lives in me, that is, in my sinful nature I want to do what is right, but I can't. (Romans 7:18 NLT)

We must stand firm on the word of God and know that God can handle what we consider being monumental disasters in our lives. God can and will handle it for us if we let Him. But we miss the mark when we ask God for help and then turn right around and run to man for help. By doing this, we strip the power from God's hands and put our trust in man who has no power. Now understand what I'm saying here, God still has the power to deliver us, but because we've chosen to override His power and authority He simply removes Himself from the equation. There's no point of God continuing to work on our behalf because we've taken the petition from Him and given it to man who has no power. Satan does not hold the keys to victory! God does!

When we put our complete faith in God, we win. We must submit our will to the will of God. God wants to deliver you but you must trust Him and Him alone to do just that. Stop playing with the enemy. He can't save you. He can't deliver you. He won't jump in the fire with you; instead he will allow you to be burned and consumed. You cannot trust the enemy. Give your burdens to the Lord and leave them there. Be confident in God's abilities. God said He would never leave nor forsake us and He's proven that time and time again. Satan can't promise you that.

His job is to lure and bait you and once he has you where he wants you he will abandon you. But God is with us always. Put your trust and confidence in God.

Put not your trust in princes, nor in the son of man, in whom there is no help. (Psalms 146:3 KJV)

You cannot trust the flesh. The flesh is a mess and it will mess you up if you don't allow God complete control. The flesh will fail you every time. But God always does what he says. He will never fail you. Stop running to men for answers. God has the answer to every question; the solution to every problem; the cure for every disease. Everything you need is wrapped up and tied up in God. Stop trying to figure it out on your own. Stop trying to fix your own problems. Let God be God in your life. God is not like man. He's unable to lie to you and he will never need to repent. Trust God! Stop scheming, plotting and planning your way out and let God bring you out. Don't depend on your mental capabilities. Trust God!

Trust in the LORD with all thine heart; and lean not unto thine own understanding. [6]In all thy ways acknowledge him, and he shall direct thy paths. (Proverbs 3:5-6 KJV)

Putting your trust and confidence in man negates your belief in God. You cannot truly believe that God exist when your trust is not in Him. There are consequences that accompany putting your trust in man. When you remove God from the situation all you're left with is a bigger mess. Nothing will go right. You will only dig a deeper ditch and before long you will fall in it. At that moment you'll realize that you really do need the Lord. You will realize that God is the only one that can deliver you out of the snare of the enemy. Don't worsen your situation by trying to do things your way. It must be God's way or no way. Why seek victory in man when God is Victory? Why go to man for answers when God is the only answer? Why seek the opinion of man when the only opinion that matters is God? You waste precious time when you put your faith in the wrong source. Let God be God!

PRAYER OF EMPOWERMENT:

Father, I put my complete trust in you. I know that you are the only one that can save, set free and deliver. My faith is in you and you alone. I trust you to do what is best for me. Thank you for being my shelter from the storm. Thank you for being the rock of my salvation. Thank you for being my Jehovah Jireh. Thank you for protecting me and dispatching your angels to watch over me. Empower me to continue to put my complete confidence in you. Thank you for being lord over my life. Thank you for never leaving me; never forsaking me; never leaving my seed begging for bread. Empower me to continue walking by faith and not by what I see. Thank you for always being available to me. I will forever trust you and be lead by your direction. I depend on you and not my human ability. I trust your wisdom and not the opinions of man. Thank you for being my strong deliverer. I will praise you today and always. I yield my will to your will. You have full reign over my life. Amen

LAW ABIDING CITIZENS

(LIVING AN OBEDIENT LIFESTYLE)

SCRIPTURAL EMPHASIS: 1 Samuel 15:22

And Samuel said, Hath the LORD as great delight in burnt offerings and sacrifices, as in obeying the voice of the LORD? <u>Behold, to obey is better than sacrifice</u>, and to hearken than the fat of rams.

Sacrifice: destruction or surrender of something for the sake of something else: something given up or lost.

Obedience: submissive to the will of another; to submit readily to control or guidance.

Do you think all GOD wants are sacrifices— empty rituals just for show? Do you think your offerings to God are more important than your obedience to Him? What God truly desires is your obedience; your willingness to allow Him to lead and guide you. Your sacrifice means nothing if you are not walking in obedience to God.

The Bible tells us in 1 Samuel 15:22 that it is better to obey than to sacrifice. The normal view of this scripture reveals to us that it's better to heed to the voice of God than to have to endure the punishment for not doing so. As the definition above states, sacrifice causes you to surrender something for the sake of something else. Because we fail to obey God we must now endure the results of our disobedience. A sacrifice is usually something we necessarily don't want to do, but what makes our sacrifice worthy is when we do it regardless of how our flesh feels,

167

because we love the Lord more. Sacrifice in the instance of disobedience will not feel good because we have done or said something that is contrary to the word of God. When you disobey God you will be punished. There are consequences to disobeying God. Just as it is in the natural, when you disobey your parents or those that have rule over you there are consequences that result from your disobedience. You will have to endure some type of punishment or correction. I learned early in life that obedience is better than sacrifice.

If we look all throughout the Bible we can clearly see where disobedience has resulted in consequences and punishment.

Romans 5:19 tells us,

For as by one man's disobedience many were made sinners, so by the obedience of one shall many be made righteous.

Let's look at this for a moment....It only took ONE man to disobey God and the end result of his disobedience affected us all. Disobedience carries a high price tag. If it were not for God's grace and mercy many of us would be dead in our sins right now. When God instructs you to do anything, it would be in your best interest to answer the call and do whatever the task is to the best of your ability. What happens however is when we try to do things our way instead of God's way. Or we tend to do only the part that is feasible and comfortable to us. But partial obedience is still complete disobedience. You can't half do anything that God has commanded you to do and expect the promises of God to be showered on you. It doesn't work that way.

How can you say you love God, yet not obey Him? John 14:15 (Amplified) says, If you [really] love me, you will keep (obey) my commands. Verse 23-24 (Amplified) of this same chapter states, Jesus answered, If a person [really] loves me, he will keep my word [obey my teaching]; and My Father will love him, and we will come

to him and make our home (abode, special dwelling place) with him.
*[24] Anyone who does not [really] love me does not observe and obey
my teaching. And the teaching which you hear and heed is not mine,
but [comes] from the Father who sent Me.*

**What a powerful statement....If you do not obey God, you don't
love him. Our disobedience negates the love we say we have for
God. But if we walk in total obedience, not partial but total,
because again partial obedience is still disobedience, then and
only then can we proclaim our love for God. How can we say we
love God and our lives are totally opposite of His word? This is
something we all need to examine in our daily lives. Am I living
up to my confession? Do I truly love God? Am I yielding my life
to God completely?**

**Let's take a look at what happens when we yield our lives to
Christ in total submission and obedience.**

John 5:24 - *Verily, verily, I say unto you, He that heareth my word,
and believeth on him that sent me, hath everlasting life, and shall not
come into condemnation; but is passed from death unto life.*

Deuteronomy 28:1-2 - *[1] And it shall come to pass, if thou shalt
hearken diligently unto the voice of the LORD thy God, to observe
and to do all his commandments which I command thee this day, that
the LORD thy God will set thee on high above all nations of the
earth: [2] And all these blessings shall come on thee, and overtake
thee, if thou shalt hearken unto the voice of the LORD thy God.*

**Deuteronomy 28:11 tells us we will be blessed with financial
prosperity when we obey God.**

*And the LORD shall make thee plenteous in goods, in the fruit of thy
body, and in the fruit of thy cattle, and in the fruit of thy ground, in
the land which the LORD sware unto thy fathers to give thee.*

Joshua 1:8 tells us we will be blessed with success for our obedience.

This book of the law shall not depart out of thy mouth; but thou shalt meditate therein day and night, that thou mayest observe to do according to all that is written therein: for then thou shalt make thy way prosperous, and then thou shalt have good success.

Proverbs 10:27 tells us our days will be long if we are obedient to God.

The fear of the LORD prolongeth days: but the years of the wicked shall be shortened.

These are just a few of the blessings and promises of God if we walk in obedience. The most important promise is that we will obtain eternal life if we obey God. Obedience to God shows your love for God.

PRAYER OF EMPOWERMENT:

Father, forgive us for our disobedience and neglect of your word. Forgive us for even thinking we stand in right fellowship with you when our lives are contrary to your word. Lord, deliver us from ourselves. Teach us how to obey your word. Forgive us Father for our shortcomings. Strengthen us to walk in obedience. Let our sacrifice be that of praise, glory and honor to you. Help us to submit our will to your will. Lord we give you complete control; lead us and guide us into all truth. Teach us to not be weary in well doing, for we know we shall reap if we faint not.

Amen.

"STAY IN THE SHIP"

SCRIPTURAL EMPHASIS:

Paul said to the centurion and to the soldiers, except these abide in the ship, ye cannot be saved. (Acts 27:31 KJV)

It is so easy to abandon and jump ship in the crux of turbulent storms, test and trials that accompany life. Some choose to surrender in the midst of adversity instead of holding on to their belief and faith in God. Some give up hope of being delivered because of what their physical eyes reveal. Instead of focusing on the problem solver, they focus on the problem which begins to eat away and disintegrate their faith. But the word of God tells us we must endure hardness as a good soldier. We cannot become entangled with the affairs of this life.

Thou therefore endure hardness, as a good soldier of Jesus Christ. 4 No man that warreth entangleth himself with the affairs of this life; that he may please him who hath chosen him to be a soldier. (2 Timothy 2:3-4 KJV)

We must stand up under the pressures and persecutions of life. We must be strong and vigilant when we are faced with tests, trials and temptations. We are to be watchful and mindful during our time of affliction and persecution.

But watch thou in all things, endure affliction. (2 Timothy 4:5a KJV)

No matter how difficult our journey becomes, no matter how rough the trial, we must stand firm on the word of God and our faith in Him. It was never promised that this Christian walk would be easy, but Christ promised that He would never leave us, nor would he ever forsake us or leave our seed begging bread. He promised to be with us always. God is with us through torrential rains; He's with us through the fire: He's with us through every test and trial. God is with us, but we must stand firm and not waiver in our belief. We must have a determination to stand. We as Christians will face opposition; we will face persecution; we will face adversity; we will face afflictions, but we must stand. God promised us that He would deliver us out of them all.

Many are the afflictions of the righteous: but the LORD delivereth him out of them all. (Psalms 34:19 KJV)

It's key to note that the Lord said He will deliver us "out of" and not from. This lets us know that we will be faced with affliction, persecution, tests, trials and temptations. We will not be exempt from these things, but His promise is that He will deliver us "out" of them all. Don't jump ship. If you jump ship you will not survive. Stay in the ship. Our tests and trials come to make us strong. We become wiser when we face adversity. They don't come to tear us down but to build us up. God wants to know that He can trust you when things are going well and when things are falling apart. He wants to know that He can trust you when you have money in the bank and when you don't have a dime. He wants to know that He can trust you through the good and the bad. Stay in the ship.

Your tests will produce testimonies. You can't help or encourage your brothers and sisters in the gospel to endure if you're always throwing in the towel and waving the white flag of surrender. You must abide in the ship and endure. Paul was able to exhort Timothy to endure hardness because of his endurance to the issues and adversities of life. Paul knew how to endure hardness.

He knew how to go through a test. He didn't cave in or give up but he endured. Paul was stoned, beaten, and evicted, but he never gave up. He was thrown in jail, beaten with many stripes but he still managed to erect songs of praise. He didn't sit in a pool of tears feeling sorry for himself. No, on the contrary he pushed beyond the pain and gave God praise. He pushed beyond the tests and birthed a testimony.

God has you in the furnace of life because He refining you. He's burning off everything that is contrary to His perfect will for your life. He has you in the storms of life, because He's producing endurance and perseverance. He wants to see that you can endure the suffering. He wants to know if you can praise in pain. What you need to survive abides in the ship. If you jump overboard you will die.

There are seven things in the ship that is vital to our walk with Christ. Let's take a closer look.

#1 There is Companionship in the ship. We are not alone. God is right there with us in the midst of our tests and trials.

I know the LORD is always with me. I will not be shaken, for he is right beside me. (Psalms 16:8 NLT)

I am a companion of all who fear you, of those who keep your precepts. (Psalms 199:63 ESV)

#2 There is Relationship in the ship. God wants us to have a relationship with Him not just a few meaningless encounters. He wants us to know Him.

[For my determined purpose is] that I may know Him [that I may progressively become more deeply and intimately acquainted with Him, perceiving and recognizing and understanding the wonders of His Person more strongly and more clearly], and that I may in that same way come to know the power out flowing from His resurrection

[[a]which it exerts over believers], and that I may so share His suffering as to be continually transformed [in spirit into His likeness even] to His death, [in the hope]

[11]That if possible I may attain to the [[b]spiritual and moral] resurrection [that lifts me] out from among the dead [even while in the body]. (Philippians 3:10-11 Amplified)

#3 There is Discipleship in the ship. God has called us to be His disciples. In order to be a Disciple of Christ one must first have a spirit of repentance and walk in the integrity of a steward. We must continuously pattern our lives after the example and teachings of Christ.

Jesus came and told his disciples, "I have been given all authority in heaven and on earth. [19] Therefore, go and make disciples of all the nations,[a] baptizing them in the name of the Father and the Son and the Holy Spirit. [20] Teach these new disciples to obey all the commands I have given you. And be sure of this: I am with you always, even to the end of the age." (Matthew 28:18-20 NLT)

#4 There is Fellowship in the ship. God desires to commune with us. He desires that we commune with him. Believers should always fellowship with other believers because it strengthens the cords that bind. There is power in numbers, especially when everyone is on one accord and operating according to the spirit and authority of God.

A person standing alone can be attacked and defeated, but two can stand back-to-back and conquer. Three are even better, for a triple-braided cord is not easily broken. (Ecclesiastes 412 NLT)

#5 There is Partnership in the ship. God desires us to partner with Him. He wants us to connect with Him. When you're connected to the power source there's nothing you cannot attain.

Two people are better off than one, for they can help each other succeed. [10] If one person falls, the other can reach out and help. But someone who falls alone is in real trouble. (Ecclesiastes 4:9-10 NLT)

God will do this, for he is faithful to do what he says, and he has invited you into partnership with his Son, Jesus Christ our Lord. (1 Corinthians 1:9 NLT)

#6 There is Mentorship in the ship. God desires to mentor us. He longs for us to sit at His feet and learn of Him. He equips us with the essential tools required to walk upright before Him. He trains us to go out and train and impart wisdom and knowledge in others.

You have heard me teach things that have been confirmed by many reliable witnesses. Now teach these truths to other trustworthy people who will be able to pass them on to others. (2 Timothy 2:2 NLT)

#7 There is Friendship in the ship. God desires to be our friend. We should desire to be a friend of God. Our desire should be that God has counted us worthy enough to call us friend. God is the best friend anyone could ever and will ever have in life. He's a friend that will not lie to you, steal from you, cheat on you, or abandon you. He will always be there when you need a shoulder to cry on. He will answer when you call. He's the only friend that you can totally and completely trust.

You are my friends if you do what I command.(John 15:14 NLT)

One who has unreliable friends soon comes to ruin, but there is a friend who sticks closer than a brother. (Proverbs 18:24 NIV)

So as you can see, everything you need is in the ship. Don't jump overboard. Don't weigh the ship down with pity parties and woe is me stories. Throw negativity and doubt overboard. Throw unhealthy relationships overboard. Throw unbelief overboard.

Throw depression, oppression, recession and digression overboard. But stay in the ship. In the ship is where you will find life. Hope, peace, love and soundness of mind is in the ship. Deliverance and salvation is in the ship. Praise through your pain. Remember that as long as you are abiding in God and He is abiding in you there is nothing more you need. The bible tells us that even in the event of temptation that God has already provided us with a plan of escape. So stay in the ship and heed to the voice of God. Weeping only endures for a night; in the morning you will find joy.

PRAYER OF EMPOWERMENT:

Father, we thank you for being ever present with us. We thank you for not leaving or forsaking us in the midst of life's trials, tests, persecutions, adversity and persecutions. Lord, we thank you for revealing to us that we have Companionship, Relationship, Friendship, Discipleship, Partnership, Fellowship and Mentorship as long as we abide in you and you in us. Empower us to empower others to hold on in the face of trials and temptations. Lord, strengthen us to hold on to your loving embrace and not surrender in defeat. Thank you for giving us the essential tools and guidance to overcome every obstacle that we may face. Father, we thank you and we bless your holy name. Amen.

It is my prayer that this book has blessed, inspired, uplifted, enlightened, motivated, challenged and strengthened you. Thank you for taking the time to read what has been imparted to me through the Holy Spirit. I pray the abundant blessings of God over your life and that you will prosper even as your soul prospers.

Sandra S. Williams

www.ingramcontent.com/pod-product-compliance
Lightning Source LLC
Chambersburg PA
CBHW032119040426

42449CB00005B/194